IMPROVING PROFESSIONAL LEARNING

IMPROVING PROFESSIONAL LEARNING

Twelve Strategies to Enhance Performance

Alan B. Knox

Foreword by Ronald M. Cervero

Routledge
Taylor & Francis Group

NEW YORK AND LONDON

First published 2016 by Stylus Publishing, LLC.

First Edition, 2016

Published 2023 by Routledge
605 Third Avenue, New York, NY 10017
4 Park Square, Milton Park, Abingdon, Oxon OX14 4RN

Routledge is an imprint of the Taylor & Francis Group, an informa business

Library of Congress Cataloging-in-Publication Data
Names: Knox, Alan B. (Alan Boyd), 1931-
Title: Improving professional learning : 12 strategies to enhance performance
  / Alan B. Knox.
Description: First edition. | Sterling, Virginia : Stylus Publishing, LLC, [2016] | Includes bibliographical references and index.
Identifiers: LCCN 2015022254|
ISBN 9781620363638 (cloth) |
ISBN 9781620363645 (pbk.) |
Subjects: LCSH: Professional education. | Continuing education. | Career development. | Educational leadership.
Classification:LCCLC1059.K662016|DDC370.71/1--dc23
LC record available at http://lccn.loc.gov/2015022254

ISBN 13: 978-1-62036-363-8 (hbk)
ISBN 13: 978-1-62036-364-5 (pbk)
ISBN 13: 978-1-00-344526-5 (ebk)

DOI: 10.4324/9781003445265

CONTENTS

FOREWORD

A central feature of societies in the twentieth century was the professionalization of their workforces with nearly 25% of the U.S. workforce, for example, being classified as professionals. These professionals include teachers, physicians, clergy, lawyers, social workers, nurses, business managers, psychologists, and accountants. Educational systems have been a key feature of this professionalization project, and, consequently, substantial financial and human resources have been deployed to support three to six years of professionals' initial education. Until the 1960s, many leaders in the professions believed that these years of preservice education, along with some refreshers, were sufficient for a lifetime of work. However, with rapid social changes, explosion of research-based knowledge, and spiraling technological innovations, these leaders now recognize the need to continually prepare people for 40 years of professional practice through continuing education.

As these systems of continuing education have been built over for the past 50 years and into the twenty-first century, scholars and leaders have noted the similarities of the continuing education efforts of individual professions in terms of goals, processes, and structures. Thus, the concept of "continuing professional education" began to be used in the late 1960s, with the rationale being that the understanding of similarities and differences across the professions would yield a fresh exchange of ideas, practices, and solutions to common problems. A central problem that has been the subject of much discussion and research in continuing professional education is that those who lead and teach in these formal educational programs are experts in the subject matter of their profession but haven't been prepared to lead the learning activities of those who participate in the programs. Thus, the participants fail to be engaged in an optimal learning activity that could potentially improve their professional performance.

Alan B. Knox has written *Improving Professional Learning: Twelve Strategies to Enhance Performance* to provide tools for leaders to solve this problem. He has been among the key scholars providing leadership for this important area of scholarship and practice for decades and has coalesced all of his insights, experiences, and research to help educational leaders improve professional learning. As a reader, you will find that this book is jam-packed with immediately useful insights in each of the 12 chapters in part one. If you are in an organizational leadership position, the book would be a great resource for the professional development of your learning activity leaders. If you are a learning activity leader, any one of the 12 chapters can be read individually or collectively to provide guidance as you plan or deliver the activity. The advice that Knox provides in each chapter is well-organized with real examples (many of which I have experienced) and clear guidance on best practices, with a set of key references that you can follow-up with if you desire additional information.

The 12 strategies that form the heart of this book are essential elements for anyone providing professional learning, from starting where the learner is, through the focus on active learning, and ending with providing feedback to learners and other stakeholders. Knox wisely doesn't provide you with a recipe to follow in lock-step fashion, but, rather, recognizes the nuances of the leader-learner interaction in a complex environment. This is, indeed, a refreshing and realistic approach to leading professional learning. In a sense, the book practices what it preaches by serving as a tool for the professional development of the leaders of professional learning. The book concludes with an excellent bibliographic essay on the evidence-base for each of the 12 strategies for those readers who wish to continue with their own professional learning.

Without a doubt, this book is a major contribution to the support of improved practice of professional learning and continuing professional education. Its tightly-woven set of 12 strategies, numerous practical examples, and evidence-based guidance provide activity leaders the intellectual and practical tools to engage learners optimally to strengthen performance and quality improvement. This book was written from a unique vantage point, as Knox has been an important leader and scholar preparing thousands of educators in person and through his books for decades. Only he could have written this book, and we are very fortunate that he devoted his talent to this important project.

Ronald M. Cervero, PhD
Professor and Associate Vice President for Instruction
University of Georgia

PREFACE

This book provides basic guidelines to enhance the efforts of the millions of people in various professional fields who coordinate and guide professional learning activities each year. Given the increasing complexity and rapid pace of change in our world, lifelong learning has become essential, not only for those in the helping professions but also for those they serve. After many decades of experience in planning, conducting, and studying professional development activities, I've accumulated thousands of examples, many included in practical plans and reports as well as publications regarding professional learning activities, based on research and evaluation studies. In the course of recent projects in the field of adult and continuing education, I recognized the value of analyzing these examples to help those involved in professional learning make the most of their educational activities.

The guidelines for effective leadership of activities pertain to all professions, especially the helping professions such as teaching, health care, faith communities, counseling, libraries, and social work. Improving performance by helping professionals also includes enhancing the learning and performance of their students, patients, members, and clients. Thus, investments of time and money in effective professional development activities can pay rich dividends by enhancing workplace performance and quality of life for those who participate in professional learning activities as well as for the people they serve.

This book provides lessons learned from my analysis of many examples from various professional fields. I conclude that there are basic guidelines that can help explain the disparities between the most effective and least effective sessions. Each professional field has specialized content that is basic to excellent professional performance. Aside from distinctive content and topics central to each professional field, the guidelines are about program leadership and the process of helping professionals learn and enhance their performance.

The chapters combine evidence-informed concepts with practical examples to enable readers to develop some high-priority guidelines to improve interactive professional learning activities conducted by associations, enterprises, and educational institutions. The concepts and examples illustrate how activity leaders can estimate and guide the personal and situational influences on professional education and performance. The chapters also illustrate how professional activity leaders and coordinators can improve the effectiveness of the participants' learning experience.

The process and benefits of effective learning activities include shared leadership among program coordinators, leaders, participants, and other stakeholders. Many effective professional learning activities use combinations of face-to-face and technology-based learning activities. As a result, leaders of very effective professional learning activities discover concepts and procedures that enable them to deal with this collaborative learning process and achieve outstanding results. These educators from various professional fields also learn about the creative process from each other as a result of increasing instances of interprofessional education and collaborative performance.

In the spirit of practicing what you teach, the brief summaries of leadership tasks beginning on page 5 of the introduction can help readers select which of the 12 chapters they find most relevant. Each of the chapters illustrates features of one or a series of effective professional learning activities. The chapters begin with a leadership task for an activity session and an example, followed by a sequence of concepts and additional authentic examples from various professional fields, questions prompting reflections about applying the information to each leader's session, and a suggested selection of guidelines to enhance leadership of future sessions. The book concludes with a bibliographic essay and a reference list for readers interested in deepening their understanding and their leadership of some tasks.

Improving Professional Learning and Performance

L eaders in various professional fields appreciate the importance of career-long professional learning. They recognize that effectively guiding professional learning sessions is central to strengthening performance and quality improvement. The suggested guidelines for creative learning activities included in this book can enhance the efforts of session leaders, participants, and coordinators.

Effective leadership of learning is central to more effective professional performance. At best, such activities can be creative experiences for session participants, leaders, coordinators, and other stakeholders as they share in planning, conducting, and evaluating the process and outcomes. The intended results typically include improved professional performance, quality improvement, and benefits for the people served by helping professionals. Intended results also include enhanced learning and performance by the students, patients, clients, and members in fields such as health care, education, faith communities, counseling, social work, library science, and community development, and those who are the intended beneficiaries of helping professionals who participate in learning activities throughout their careers.

This book is based on creative teaching and learning. Excellent educational transactions between teaching and learning are similar to other creative activities in which participants have a transcendent experience that expands beyond their past personal activities. Effective leaders are prepared to help adults learn and enhance their knowledge, skills, and attitudes for improved performance in the workplace. The 12 brief chapters on activity leader tasks are each focused on selected guidelines to reduce complexity for readers who may have limited familiarity with concepts about guiding creative learning activities. The chapters explain how and why professional learning leaders can gradually enhance the abilities and commitments of participants and other stakeholders so that learning activities are creative experiences that enable improved performance of helping professionals and the people they serve. The concepts, examples, and tasks in each chapter prepare readers for the complexity of guiding learning, so that participants and leaders can experience the creative flow of inquiry and enhanced performance together.

In addition to the participants, leaders who guide the activities, and the coordinators who help them, other stakeholders include administrators from the sponsoring organization (enterprise, association, educational institution), funders that contribute resources, and representatives of cooperating organizations. Winning and maintaining cooperation from such stakeholders calls for additional types of creativity from leaders and coordinators. As interprofessional cooperation has increased, so have examples of interprofessional learning activities. Because of the loosely coupled connections among the stakeholders, each interaction is an opportunity for decision and discovery. Effective leaders invest their time and thought in shared leadership to achieve multiple returns in the form of mutually beneficial exchanges among stakeholders that contribute to creative activities and desirable results in enhanced professional performance.

Because each professional field and related publications use distinctive *content* (words, concepts, symbols, and terminology to communicate specialized ideas about the profession), the following generic terms and definitions are used to encourage interprofessional cooperation: *activity* (any one or a series of educational programs, sessions, or events), *leader* (one or more people who guide learning activities as presenters, faculty, trainers, mentors, supervisors, or specialists), *coordinators* (people who select and assist activity leaders on behalf of the provider organization), *provider* (the association, enterprise, or educational organization that provides professional learning opportunities), *resource people* (experts regarding content, technology, or evaluation who help leaders and participants), *stakeholders* (people in various roles who have a stake in the session, such as administrators, leaders, coordinators, participants, funders, and cosponsors), *those served* (people who benefit directly from assistance by activity participants in their life roles, such as students, patients, members, clients, and patrons), *resources* (such as money and volunteer leaders that coordinators seek to enhance sessions), *expectations* (combinations of personal aspirations and short-term expectations about progress), and *proficiencies* (combinations of knowledge, skills, and attitudes that constitute capabilities to perform, given the opportunity). These definitions and distinctions are further developed in this introduction, in the 12 chapters, and in the bibliographic essay.

Adults mainly become who they are based on their interpretation of their experience. Young people and adults develop implicit and largely unexamined priorities and criteria for important decisions. A combination of personal and situational influences contributes to increasing diversity during the life cycle. The basic concept for leaders of learning activities is to be responsive and to provide options for diverse adult participants, which is essential for the provision of effective educational opportunities for adults.

With each new experience, adults recall related knowledge, skills, and attitudes. Their evolving sense of self is based on their experiences, along with their observations, readings, and media interactions. At each stage of the life cycle, their sense of self shapes their performance in their roles in family, work, health, and community. Their past and future performances are guided by personal preferences for combinations of continuity and change.

Changing goals and expectations trigger adult inquiry, learning, and exploration, during which people draw on recall and reconstructed memories. Some people engage in reflection to transcend narrow personalization through analysis of similarities and differences to appreciate their interdependence and to achieve greater well-being and inner peace. This clarification of their hierarchy of values helps them focus on essential priorities. An important contribution of parents, mentors, teachers, and other people who guide adult learning is to help participants clarify their priorities and guidelines for the decisions they make. Because of the ever-changing facts about life, the secret of life is the ongoing process of lifelong learning.

Leaders of creative learning activities benefit from these developmental concepts of experience and personal and situational influences in the face of increasing diversity and the importance of reflection. Activity leaders and coordinators use such concepts to plan, conduct, and evaluate a sequence of active learning opportunities. Effective leaders who understand these developmental concepts are armed with questions to ask about specific participants and the stakeholders with whom they interact.

Wise leaders enable participants to deepen their comprehension of program content as it relates to their role performance. Such content usually includes generalizations from organized knowledge about categories of people, such as concepts, facts, trends, and causes, which can serve as a foundation for leaders and participants to deepen their appreciation of thoughts and feelings as people interact with empathy when confronted with multiple personal and situational influences. Understanding people can deepen one's empathy and transcendence by considering others as interconnected parts of unpredictable case examples about how the world works.

The creativity of coordinators, session leaders, participants, and other program stakeholders entails guidelines for mutually beneficial exchanges and successive approximations. These joint decisions reflect stakeholder understandings of activity goals, participants' characteristics and expectations, and leader assistance with the process of planning, conducting, and evaluating a sequence of learning activities aimed at enhanced performance and quality improvement.

Additional concepts about creativity are the cornerstone of this distinctive rationale for guidelines to conduct effective professional learning activities.

Guiding creative learning activities is similar to directing performing arts events, which involves shared leadership among an ensemble of stakeholders. The central role of leaders of activity sessions is cooperation with participants and coordinators in decisions about activity purposes, guidelines, plans, desired proficiency, learning activities, and ongoing evaluation feedback to stakeholders.

Activity leaders and coordinators also seek support from administrators, funders, and policymakers who typically influence learning activities and occupational performance as well as decisions about blended forms of educational technology with participant interaction. Activity participants from the helping professions should share what they learn with the people they serve, such as students and patients. This teaching and learning method is in contrast to all too many staff development activities that are routine preplanned disseminations of content, such as "death by PowerPoint" or passive learning from technology-based curricula. The organizations, associations, and enterprises that provide educational opportunities for helping professionals attract able stakeholders, whose educational and occupational experiences allow them to volunteer to help with professional learning sessions. Features of shared leadership and responsive learning activities are similar to journal clubs'.

Effective leaders and coordinators use implicit guidelines and explicit checklists to guide program decisions and communication with each other, participants, and other stakeholders. In addition to informal understandings as these stakeholders work together, a set of standards of achievable best practice from professional fields can be used as a source for guidelines. The guidelines for each activity contribute to leader and participant alignment regarding objectives, activities, and evaluation criteria. Using guidelines to conduct creative learning activities enables the leader to include supportive and challenging interactions to facilitate participant efforts to enhance participants' professional performance during and following learning activities.

Each of the 12 chapters focuses on an important task for activity leadership and contains pertinent examples, concepts, and guidelines. However, these leadership tasks are not a series of steps. Similar to many creative activities, they are 12 interconnected components for leaders and other stakeholders to use flexibly to guide participant progress toward enhanced professional performance. This introduction concludes with a brief overview of the 12 chapters, each of which includes distinctive features of the leadership task and connections with related leadership tasks.

The following overview allows readers to focus on the leadership tasks of special interest to them, along with connections to related tasks. The book concludes with a bibliographic essay of publications listed by chapter to guide interested readers to more detailed sources and explanations.

Overview of Leadership Tasks

Establishing Shared Purposes

Effective activity leaders seek to align program goals with participants' experiences and expectations. Each learning activity typically focuses on an aspect of professional development and enhanced performance. Sources of potential program goals include achieving the purposes of a distinctive specialized professional field as well as general professional purposes (theoretical knowledge, problem solving, practical knowledge, self-enhancement, formal preparation, credentialing, communities of practice, legal reinforcement, public acceptance, ethical practice, penalties, relation to other vocations, and relation to users of service). Other sources are professional standards, emerging trends, and participant expectations in view of their past experience and future performance. Leaders and coordinators should evaluate participants' experience and expectations to reach agreement on specific objectives and activities in the advance information provided about an activity, adjustments to the activity, and how to individualize the activity.

Selecting Able Leaders

Activity effectiveness and participant progress depend on the abilities of leaders who guide the learning effort. Based on specific content, goals, and participants, various leaders can be very effective. In general, leader familiarity with professional performance can enhance responsiveness to participants. A widespread characteristic of excellent professional learning activity leaders is that they are supportive and challenging. A supportive session leader helps create a climate of trust and encouragement in which participants can explore and reflect on the implications of the activity for themselves. A leader's style can challenge participants to help them enhance their mastery and chart new directions. Experienced program developers can use criteria for leader selection and assessment along with feedback from similar past sessions. This can guide their decisions about activity purposes and leaders to fit participant performance and future improvements and reflect a combination of personal and situational influences.

Being Responsive to Participants' Experiences and Expectations

Able session leaders guide learning activities that are responsive to the personal motives and characteristics of participants. Effective leaders typically estimate participants' current proficiencies as they relate to the purpose of the session. Usual features include participants' level of content mastery, change orientation such as acceptance or resistance, communication style, self-assurance, special abilities, and what they want to gain from an activity. Awareness of participants' characteristics from similar previous activities can provide estimates that can be refined by getting to know some of the participants early in an activity. Responsiveness can also enhance helping participants' ongoing connections. During early stages, leaders can provide opportunities for participants to learn from each other and available resource people. Participants are a major source of insight to guide responsiveness during interactive activities when they share their reflections about their profession. Responsiveness can be increased by the leader's attention to expectations, motives, diversity, influences, and active learning.

Specifying Current Participant Proficiencies

Perhaps the most useful information for a leader to help participants to learn anything in professional development activities is the participant's current proficiency (combination of knowledge, skills, and attitudes). Typically, an activity's purpose is to improve a given aspect of occupational performance. Because of their professional experience and self-selection for an activity, participants usually have multiple learning abilities. One feature of a participant's current proficiency related to an activity is to estimate the combination of knowledge, skills, and attitudes he or she already has related to the aspect of performance the participant is seeking to master. The participant's self-assessment, combined with at least one additional source, can provide a sufficient estimate that can be modified in the early part of the activity. A simulation that entails analysis, creativity, and reflection can help a leader evaluate participants' current proficiency.

Developing Shared Expectations

Much of professional development is related to participants' expectations to enhance their occupational performance. Shared clarification of participants' desired proficiencies can enable leaders, participants, and other stakeholders associated with session planning to agree on ways activities can be responsive to participant's motivations, build on current proficiencies, and respond to their expectations. Several concepts and procedures are especially helpful for shared understanding. For example, making learning outcomes explicit can increase cooperation and progress by aligning participants' expectations with feasible assistance. While participants typically have multiple motives related to professional learning activities, their expectations regarding progress reflect combinations of past experience and perceived opportunities. Major changes related to a participant's profession or his or her local practice could trigger a heightened readiness to learn and change. Leaders can help participants update their expectations. Leaders who help participants make their desired proficiencies more explicit can also contribute to their mastery, motivation, and persistence in ongoing improvement in performance and benefits. Evaluations of expectations can be shared among participants, session leaders, and other stakeholders.

Addressing Gaps Between Current and Desired Proficiencies

Explicit understanding of current and desired proficiencies allows participants and other stakeholders to recognize more clearly the discrepancies between current and desired proficiencies. This understanding is very important because it serves many purposes, one of which is specifying educational needs and gaps between current and desired proficiencies. A personal inventory of proficiencies relevant to an activity's purpose can help participants appreciate the importance of continuity as well as change and build on their current expertise. Assessment of a participant's gap can encourage reflection on past influences as well as future directions of the journey. Analysis of discrepancies from multiple participants and similar members of the profession can deepen understanding of diversity, solidarity, and personal and situational influences. Reflection on the evolution of discrepancies over time can contribute to an appreciation for indigenous knowledge and values, the type of useful assistance, change events that can trigger readiness to learn, and innovation.

Analyzing Situational Influences on Performance

Some influences on professional performance extend beyond session leaders and participants. For example, each professional field has societal and organizational trends, norms, and issues that can influence opportunities and threats to consider. Such illustrative influences include shared practice standards, interprofessional performance, and increased use of educational technology. Session leaders can promote cooperation among participants with differing change orientations. Effective leaders can also help participants understand situational influences on the use of educational technology to advance professional development and quality improvement. Session leaders can recognize distinctive ways each type of provider organization can help or hinder effective activities and explore opportunities for interorganizational collaboration. Within each professional field, ongoing evaluation feedback regarding professional development and related performance, resources, and benefits can include attention to situational influences on performance.

Enhancing the Learning Transactions

The heart of professional learning activities occurs in the transactions between leaders and participants. Contributions by stakeholders and their decisions on activity context, content, participants, leaders, and outcomes come together in various transactions to enhance participant proficiency and quality of benefits to people and society. One of the many reasons such transactions are crucial for program and participant success is that interactions among participants, leaders, and other stakeholders associated with professional learning activities are enhanced by active engagement and learning. Such transactions between teaching and learning among participants and leaders can pertain to benefits and deterrents related to professional development. A transaction should be a mutually beneficial exchange. Participants in professional learning activities and the people they serve engage in seeking information and solving problems. Various stakeholders and related resources seek to help adults in these professional learning activities. In best practice, this is a symbiotic relationship. Transactions, such as building joint agendas to agree on shared objectives, case analysis, opportunities for practice, learning agreements, and evaluation feedback can be exchanges all parties can benefit from. Such exchanges can reflect connections among participants, groups, organizations, and society. Many procedures and guidelines can enable leaders to facilitate learning and change at each level and in each context. Educational technology can be used to influence access, interactions, and quality. Increasing use of simulations and virtual reality can allow participants to interact realistically, which enhances open exchange and improved performance; ongoing evaluation feedback; and exploration, planning, and improvement of transactions and professional performance.

Using Active Methods With Participants

Benefits to participants can be greatly influenced by leaders' roles and instructional methods. Activity coordinators and other stakeholders contribute to program planning and leader selection, which can be very helpful if based on familiarity with various procedures to guide active learning and quality improvement. Such concepts, combined with observing the facilitation styles of specific leaders, can help leaders focus on aspects of their interactions that help participants improve. Agreement by leaders and participants on activity purposes can enable both to connect developmental concepts to performance improvements. Various leader perspectives and teaching styles can be responsive to diverse participant experiences and what they hope to achieve. Participant inquiry, practice, and evaluation feedback take place through individual coaching, in small- and large-group activities, through organization and community development, and in relation to activity objectives and program context. Other stakeholders can contribute to the preparation of such procedures. Recruitment and retention of effective session leaders and providing opportunities for participants to engage in active learning through mutually beneficial exchanges are more likely if stakeholders make explicit their planning intentions early in the sessions.

Sequencing Activities for Progress

Effective learning events include a sequence of learning activities. Aspects of professional learning should be fostered before, during, and following an event. Career-long professional development depends on personal responsibility and self-directed learning by participants, which are subject to positive and negative influences. Some concepts and activities for educational improvement are especially important early, partway, and toward the end of one or a series of sessions. Early agreements on educational objectives, distributed opportunities for practice, and ongoing evaluation feedback are especially important. Participants' analysis and reflection about actual or simulated professional performance is also important for continued professional learning and quality improvement.

Providing Evaluation Feedback to Stakeholders

Providing ongoing evaluation feedback to stakeholders is essential for effective professional learning. Program evaluation pertains to each of the other guidelines for professional development because each leadership task can be assessed. Evaluative judgments reflect values and ethics as well as descriptions of the educational process and content. Members of the profession who are familiar with international practice settings may gain additional insights that can improve their own performance. It is important for activity leaders, participants, and other stakeholders to be engaged in planning, conducting, and providing ongoing evaluation for purposes of planning, improvement, and accountability. Fortunately, an increasing amount of information about guidelines and procedures for program evaluation is available. Interpretation and use of qualitative and quantitative evaluation results require commitment and resources from multiple stakeholders.

Recognizing Contextual Influences

Contextual influences affect professional performance and learning activities. Effective leaders help participants and other stakeholders understand the types of influences, their importance, and their implications for useful activities that enable participants to understand such influences. These influences include program image, deterrents to progress, attraction of additional participants, retention of current disciplines, extent of participation, application of knowledge gained from a session, providers, and collaboration with other stakeholders.

Conclusion

A review of these summaries provides an introduction to the chapters in sequence, or it can help you select the order in which you choose to read them. Each chapter provides a more detailed discussion with examples. Because each of these components is related to the rest, the part openers include brief explanations that are intended to alert the reader to a few of the major connections with concepts in other chapters. This can help leaders of a specific professional learning activity identify aspects they wish to strengthen and show why and how session leaders can involve other stakeholders in planning and implementing effective professional learning and quality improvement activities.

PART ONE

ALIGNING PARTICIPANT AND PROGRAM GOALS

Regarding the connection between chapters 1 and 2 on aligning participant and program goals: The tasks in these chapters reflect early decisions to select and orient activity leaders who help focus on topics and methods that fit program purposes and potential participant expectations.

1

ESTABLISHING SHARED PURPOSES

L eaders' and participants' purposes that are aligned contribute greatly to activity effectiveness. Professional development leaders' usual intent is to help participants achieve learning related to their performance. Such leaders' intentions may be largely implicit in the information about an activity provided for prospective participants. Information seeking and decisions about participation vary among potential participants, who are also diverse in how explicitly they recognize their own expectations. The examples and concepts in this chapter are intended to explain how and why it is important for leaders and participants to express and share their expectations early in a learning activity. Following the leader's task, an example is provided. The chapter concludes with suggested questions regarding selection of guidelines.

Task: The leader and participants state and share their expectations before and at the start of an activity.

Example: As you read this example, note the ways the program coordinator and schoolteachers who participated in their own action research projects each contributed to the alignment of the purposes of the activity. Many schoolteachers want to improve the quality of their program's process and results for their students and themselves. For years, collaborative action research has provided a potential way to do so.

Interested teachers volunteered to participate in a regional yearlong professional development activity, with the concurrence of their students, peers, and school administrators. A university school of education faculty member (and interested graduate students) served as the coordinator of this action outreach program. The program coordinator contacted the administrator of a professional development program in a large school district nearby about letting interested teachers know about the availability of this decentralized professional development opportunity.

As a part of the regular responsibilities for outreach scholarship in the coordinator's region, the coordinator and students developed and distributed information about a basic plan for teachers who were interested in developing, conducting, and evaluating a yearlong professional development activity.

Participating teachers were asked to draft their own individualized action research plan for quality improvement during the upcoming program year, focusing on an aspect of the curriculum that was of interest to them and their students. Early in the program year, the coordinator and graduate students worked with teachers by creating a clear, manageable, and individualized plan to improve a high-priority aspect of a course of study for their students. This was accomplished in a few evening meetings and electronic communications.

During most of the program year, ongoing evaluation feedback helped the coordinator to coach participating teachers, many of whom discovered a few other volunteers among participants with a similar experience and interest in their own action research project.

Toward the end of the program year, the participating teachers used ongoing evaluation (with information from the students, peers, and self-assessments) to analyze their progress and draw conclusions. Each teacher prepared a report (with categories suggested by the coordinator), to share with everyone associated with the action research project (students, peers, school administrator of professional development, coordinator). Similar action research opportunities were provided in subsequent years, with a collection of participant reports by participating teachers and analysis from the coordinator and students available for review.

This example illustrates teachers focusing on the primary purpose of teaching elementary and secondary school students and several other professional purposes such as problem solving, practical knowledge, self-enhancement, community of practice, and relations to students. But in what ways were coordinator and participants aligned? How about the coordinator and students who reviewed and provided feedback regarding the teacher's individualized action plans during the year?

Several additional concepts help clarify the fundamental purpose of professional development. Members of each profession are expected to continue to learn and improve their performance throughout their career; they typically expect this of themselves. This expectation can be shared by people in various roles who have a stake in the quality of professional performance.

Other stakeholders are members of organizations such as a university, an association, or an enterprise who are connected with the preparation and occupational performance of professionals. In the previous example, the school of education faculty member who served as coordinator of the professional development activity illustrated a mutually beneficial exchange between the participating teachers and the coordinator and students.

Additional stakeholders are from organizations that approve professionals to practice or who are members of related occupations. Perspectives of these and other stakeholders usually reflect their values regarding professional development and help shape their contributions to planning, conducting, and evaluating professional development activities. Clarifying alignment of purposes can contribute to session effectiveness by emphasizing shared commitment.

Most professional development and quality improvement activities are intended to help members of a profession and their work associates focus on and pursue desirable improvements in their performance and their contributions to their profession. Excellent professional performance has many topics related to standards, along with personal and situational influences on quality standards in the occupational setting. Leaders' explicit efforts to align participants and their own purposes can enhance the process.

National organizations and associations have increased their emphasis on standards and procedures for improving the quality of preparatory and continuing professional education in various professional fields such as teaching and nursing. Examples include Carnegie Foundation for the Advancement of Teaching, National Board for Professional Teaching Standards, and the Baldridge Performance Excellence Program in the U.S. Department of Commerce.

Especially for professional development session leaders interested in interprofessional education and performance, publications from such national initiatives can be a valuable source of standards that span many separate specialties. Such broad standards and criteria promote leadership on behalf of performance excellence and continuous improvement, which can be applied to local activities that have very specific missions and values.

The next example is applicable to the social work profession, for which a major aspect of its distinctive purpose is helping people learn. It illustrates features of an activity that can contribute to the clarification of a distinctive professional purpose as a shared goal. This is especially so for leaders of professional development activities as they consider activity influences, content, standards, goals, procedures, and outcomes.

Ideally, such leaders interact with pertinent stakeholders (experts, participants, technology specialists, funders, and policymakers) to plan activities that enhance participants' understanding and performance, including clarification of and commitment to a distinctive professional purpose.

Exemplary professional development activities focus on specific connections between excellent performance and selected personal and situational influences. Leaders' use of simulations, demonstrations, and other interactive methods enable participants to appreciate, practice, and receive feedback on procedures that contribute to excellent performance. This may entail explicit planning and implementation focused on standards and problem solving relevant to specific procedures, such as mentoring and case management.

For other aspects of performance, program activities help participants discover how to enhance their innovation, creativity, and results that reflect achievable standards of best practice. Professional development and quality improvement activities have limited influence on actual professional performance in the workplace. However, the purpose of effective activities can be to increase participant commitment and capacity by creating a supportive and challenging climate for learning, focusing on achievable standards of best practice, obtaining agreement on intended outcomes, providing opportunities to practice in order to increase mastery, and including feedback from ongoing evaluation.

Professional development can contribute in various ways to clarifying and emphasizing the distinctive purpose of the professional field. Doing so also helps participants understand the contribution of professional learning activities that benefit social workers and their clients.

The following example of a health profession activity illustrates several contributions of these learning activities.

> The leader set a conversational tone and urged participant commitment to high standards of professional performance, including successive stages of maintenance of competence. An accompanying PowerPoint presentation clearly listed standards, goals, and criteria for continued maintenance of competence related to credentials and certification.
>
> Participants were encouraged to ask questions throughout the session, arrange for a mentor to assist their professional development, and share their case examples of documented performance for critique and feedback. The leader responded to participant questions throughout with patience, humor, tips, and explanations regarding professional standards and related evaluation criteria.
>
> Also mentioned were available resources and assistance for ongoing professional development such as live and technology-based sessions, print and electronic publications, and guides and templates related to criteria of excellence. These options accommodated participants with diverse preferred learning styles.
>
> During a lively discussion of technical procedures, other topics were mentioned, including the potential tension between public preferences and

professional standards, alternative types of clinical technology related to participants' decision making, resistance to cooperation among specialties, and avoidance of mistakes.

During the final half hour of the activity, five contrasting case examples were reviewed. This gave the leader an opportunity to ask participants for their analyses of the case and to offer supplementary comments to reinforce the importance of individual and team commitment to excellence.

Which aspects of the foregoing example most relate to leader and participant purposes? How does an explicit focus on professional standards and excellence benefit from and contribute to alignment of purposes?

Another type of a shared purpose in a learning activity is understanding globalization. Globalization has a powerful but diffuse influence on professional learning with its increasing marketing and international movements of goods, services, and information. Such aspects related to professional development include use of communication technology, increased multicultural populations that affect social cohesion and sense of identity, and updating knowledge systems that produce knowledge workers. Global migration occurs everywhere, from poorer regions and entire nations to wealthier ones.

The negative local consequences include increased instability, poverty, illness, and hunger, as well as insufficient access to water contribute to despair and conflict, which in turn feed violent fundamentalism. Potential positive influences on professional development include appreciation of non-Western perspectives on collective as well as individual use of knowledge; holistic recognition of proficiencies composed of attitudes and skills as well as knowledge; and commitment to interconnected lifelong, lifewide, humanist learning to know, do, and cooperate.

Examples of change connected with all life roles and settings that have implications for leaders of professional development activities include responsiveness toward multiple stakeholders (faculty, professionals, related occupations, policymakers, and the people and communities that professionals serve); reflection on organizational and societal influences on professional performance and development; and awareness, engagement, and collective learning in action (such as learning communities, interprofessional practice and education, and collaboration among providers of professional development). Session leaders who help participants recognize the importance of globalization as a central purpose of the session can enable them to discover such complex connections.

Agreement among leaders and participants on activity purposes contributes to active learning during one or a series of sessions and to recognition of external influences on the activity. For example, participant progress toward increased mastery and improved performance can be enhanced when both participants and leaders share examples, questions, and explanations. Such lively case discussions can include frequent connections between important concepts and action decisions.

This can encourage participants to reflect on similarities and differences between the examples and simulations discussed in the learning activity and applications in their work setting. A desired result is greater creativity and professional innovation, which can lead to increased collaboration among professionals in the workplace and related organizations. Explicit agreement on the activity's scope and objectives can enhance appreciation of professional standards and organizational influences. Clear articulation of a learning activity's connections to broad organizational and societal issues can help attract resources and reduce deterrents to progress. This is very helpful in preparing proposals for cooperation on innovative projects. Using an exchange model of marketing concepts regarding mutual benefits can enhance leader interactions with participants that are responsive to learners' educational needs aligned with session objectives and the purposes of the provider.

The foregoing discussion and examples suggest some of the ways professional learning leaders and their stakeholders can conduct activities and emphasize the central purpose of the profession. Guidelines included here are to clarify shared purposes early, connect general performance improvement goals to shared purposes, analyze and address reasons for resistance to cooperation, include stakeholders in the clarification process, emphasize creativity and diversity as aspects of a shared purpose, consider personal and situational influences, and encourage ongoing pursuit of shared purposes beyond learning activities.

In your own professional development activities, how do you address specific learning objectives, with appropriate attention to other basic professional purposes? Which concepts in the chapter suggest promising ways to help participants relate their specific proficiencies to broader professional purposes?

Your reflections on the following questions regarding shared purposes can lead to your own guidelines for initiatives in a specific professional setting:

1. What are ways to estimate, before or early in an activity, a desirable alignment between program objectives and participant expectations?
2. How can ongoing evaluation feedback to activity stakeholders be enhanced by the use of explicitly stated shared purposes? What assessment procedures would contribute information related to responsiveness to participants' learning needs, influences on activity analysis, and use of conclusions to improve professional performance?

3. How might alignment of relevant stakeholder connections with activities contribute to future recognition and implementation of innovative and beneficial cooperation related to a shared purpose?

4. What tailored communication content and process should be considered to win and maintain engagement related to a shared program purpose by policymakers, administrators, peers, and people served by professionals? Why are opportunities for decentralization and individualization of participant engagement in professional development activities important? What contribution would be made by clear agreement on learning purposes?

5. What are desirable connections among influences on performance, program planning, shared purposes, focus on improved performance, and major program decisions?

6. What future synergistic energy could be generated through early alignment of program objectives and participants' expectations? How might explicit agreement on activity purposes by able leaders and participants help explore such opportunities?

2

SELECTING ABLE LEADERS

uiding effective learning activities depends on the abilities and dispo-
sitions of the leaders of the sessions. A basic responsibility of professional learning activity coordinators is the selection and development
of effective leaders. The purpose of this chapter is to provide concepts and
examples that can contribute to a staffing rationale for coordinators, including suggested criteria for leader selection and assessment.

The preparation and use of selection criteria may reflect various stakeholder contributions such as, for example, a diverse advisory committee
composed of practitioners, scholars, activity leaders, and participants. Selection criteria may also be used by potential leaders as a program guide and by
coordinators who select likely candidates from the applicants.

After a brief statement of the leadership task, there is an example from
the helping professions, followed by various pertinent concepts and some
additional examples. The chapter concludes with suggested questions regarding selection of guidelines.

Task: Use criteria to select and orient able leaders of professional learning
activities.

Example: A university professional school with a scientific and technical mission had, for years, conducted a large outreach distance education program.
The program coordinator was very familiar with similar outreach programs
in other states and countries. The participants were administrators in human
resource development and quality improvement (HRD) in enterprises with
many employees in technical and scientific occupations.

Some of these administrators enrolled in a certificate program with two
objectives: improving human resource development and training procedures
in the enterprise and improving the use of educational technology. The

---

participants' study and use of distance education procedures contributed to their proficiency and that of the HRD staff in their enterprise whom they assist through distance education procedures. The session leader was selected in part because of familiarity with diverse programs.

A basic question for program coordinators and other professional learning stakeholders is, What are especially important characteristics of mentors who guide learning activities? Selection and orientation of session leaders can have a major influence on program success. Stakeholders who help plan the activity can shape general program features and resources, but it is the program leaders who contribute to a sound plan and to its implementation. Several leader characteristics, if used as explicit criteria, can aid recruitment, selection, orientation, and assistance for effective leaders.

An important criterion is leader understanding of the proficiency (combination of knowledge, skills, and attitudes) to be enhanced by one or a series of activities to improve participant performance. Such leader understanding is usually reflected in a combination of content mastery, provision of active learning procedures, and encouragement of reflection by participants. A related criterion is leader or helper familiarity with actual participant occupational performance and the major influences on it. Fortunately, when a potential leader is not available with this combination of experience and abilities, various combinations of part-time and full-time leaders can contribute the desired extent and types of expertise. A coordinator's major task is to select leaders who are likely to be successful in guiding creative professional learning activities.

The following is an example of effective leadership of a three-hour, hands-on workshop for about 40 experienced professionals by an activity leader and three helpers.

The participants began by sharing introductions and expectations, which the leader had listed as such on the workshop agenda. As part of an initial case example, the leader obtained indications of participant interest, the helpers provided examples on technical procedures and comments on collaboration, and the leader explained why some procedures were used. The leader then provided an overview of a case example that prompted interaction among participants on their experiences and options and then used a set of slides to review the sequence of major steps when starting to use unfamiliar technical equipment.

After a break, three or four participants sat at small tables to use equipment and materials that were prepared for a simulation. Demonstrations, practice, and observations included use of a vertical camera and projector with a large screen to allow participants to review and comment on individual projects they were working on and the procedures they used. A similar segment of the session followed for a another procedure, which related explanations and responses to participant questions and reflections on their own assumptions and beliefs.

The leader and helpers concluded the session with comments about making revisions to obtain better results, avoiding mistakes, appreciating the gradual progression from novice to expert, and learning ways to be reflective about one's professional performance.

What does this brief summary of a professional learning activity illustrate regarding coordinator selection and orientation of activity leaders?

Another criterion is a leader's teaching style and methods that fit the program's objectives and participants' characteristics. Additional paired criteria are leader commitment and use of ongoing evaluation feedback to stakeholders that can contribute to participant engagement and quality improvement. How might a coordinator understand how well this professional learning activity worked to guide future selection of activity leaders?

Effective leaders can guide activities by helping participants understand professional trends and their own roles in the selection of active learning procedures most likely to enhance their mastery and improve their quality of performance. A trend that has influenced professional development is a transition in some fields from solo to large organization practices that include multiple specialties.

Activity leaders and participants can thus select from among many ways of learning a combination of methods that fit diverse participants' experience, expectations, and readiness to learn from each other and from exemplary practitioners. Available options include individual, technology-assisted, and small- and large-group activities. Also included are workshops, webinars, problem-based learning, and communities of practice.

Sequenced combinations of formats and methods are most likely to enhance professional performance and quality improvement. Able leaders enable participants to use their experience; engage in informal learning; interact with other participants; adopt innovative solutions; and reflect on assumptions, priorities, and implications for performance and guidelines.

Professional development coordinators may begin the leader selection process in various ways. A usual and desirable way is to begin by inviting an activity leader whose past performance has been outstanding for a return engagement. This can be a program coordinator's easiest selection option. However, if this occurs too quickly, there could be some missed opportunities. Not obtaining insights or thoughts from the leader, peers, and participants on which features they associate with success, or not comparing applicants who are outstanding leaders and others who may not be so outstanding, is a disadvantage.

Another missed opportunity is when a promising future activity leader is not able to assist and learn from the experience of observing and assisting an already outstanding leader. This gradual, homegrown procedure for obtaining additional leaders can be more cost-effective than the recruitment and selection of prospects who are unknown to a coordinator.

Other stakeholders associated with professional learning activities can also contribute to the recruitment, selection, orientation, and assessment of activity leaders. One advantage of obtaining new leaders is that they can bring new insights and contributions that enrich a professional learning activity.

A coordinator strategy that can contribute to excellent activity leadership is to begin not with the leader but with the professional development objectives and the participants. This can lead to reviewing the intended outcomes from professional development activities and using them for planning various program characteristics, then employing the resulting plans and specifications for desired features such as scheduling, location, and educational outcomes, as criteria for selection of technology and one or a combination of leaders likely to be effective.

With these or other ways to align program features and leader contributions, whoever contributes to leader selection can use a combination of implicit and explicit criteria. Although there are some decided advantages of making criteria explicit for purposes of decision making, belief in human possibilities, cooperation, and assessment, the influence of implicit criteria is widespread and has some benefits. For example, some aspects of excellent educational leader performance are difficult to specify and assess. This is especially true for qualitative aspects such as enthusiasm, inspiration, creativity, perseverance, and flexibility. People who have experience with potential leaders may recognize such qualitative aspects in a candidate, even though they may have difficulty expressing them in words or on rating forms. Similar evaluated judgments are used by reviewers of performance in fields such as literature and the arts.

Another important criterion is responsiveness to participants. Illustrative features of a responsive teaching style include use of options and examples for participants with diverse levels of experience, areas of mastery, and a preferred learning style. Another feature of responsiveness is allowing challenges, combined with evaluation feedback, to be an opportunity for progress.

Results of ongoing evaluations can also help clarify educational needs and the use of results for program planning, improvement, and accountability. Such features, along with attention to the stage of participants' career experience and reflection on relationships between participants' experience and program concepts, can be included in the sequence of learning activities as participants progress and increasingly contribute to active learning and application.

These concepts and examples emphasize the following basic ideas that activity coordinators and leaders can use to select and assess the people who guide creative professional learning efforts: Favor applicants who are likely to connect activity objectives with participants' expectations, encourage stakeholder contributions, consider combinations of leaders, use multiple selection criteria related to creative activities, use conclusions from past evaluation reports, emphasize stakeholder reflections on past experience and future directions, and include attention to participant benefits during and after professional learning activities.

Your reflections on the following questions about criteria for selecting able leaders can contribute to your guidelines for leader selection:

1. How might you estimate the likelihood that potential leaders and helpers will guide active learning using educational methods and technology that are aligned with activity objectives and pertinent participant characteristics?
2. What contributions should various stakeholders make to activity leader selection and assistance?
3. When might selection and continuation of excellent leaders be a satisfactory way to arrange for leaders of future activities? When might it be desirable to emphasize the development of new leaders? When might it be desirable to begin with activity features and participants and then select leaders who are well prepared to guide the process?
4. How well do potential leaders understand the aspects of professional performance that the activity should enhance?
5. How can you, and potential activity leaders, estimate participants' current and desired proficiency and occupational mastery to help the leaders focus on relevant objectives, activities, and evaluations?
6. What types of reflections about past experience, assumptions, and future directions by coordinators, leaders, and participants can be especially valuable regarding guiding creative learning sessions?
7. What are important benefits of well-aligned leadership for participants during and following learning activities?

PART TWO

RESPONDING TO PARTICIPANT EXPERIENCES, PROFICIENCIES, ASPIRATIONS, AND INFLUENCES

Regarding connections in chapters 3 through 7 on responding to participant experiences, proficiencies, aspirations, and influences: The tasks in these chapters center on estimating and clarifying participants' current and desired capabilities and influences on performance to achieve stakeholder cooperation, responsiveness, and enhanced performance.

3

BEING RESPONSIVE TO PARTICIPANTS' EXPERIENCES AND EXPECTATIONS

The central purpose of professional learning activities is to help participants improve aspects of their performance. Therefore, effective activity leaders emphasize providing methods and climates for learning that are responsive to participants' experiences and aspirations.

Able leaders emphasize responsiveness to participants and other stakeholders as they guide exploration of mutually beneficial connections between activity goals and participants' characteristics. This process tends to begin informally and become more focused and supportive as the activity progresses.

Ways to increase responsiveness include focusing on performance, recognizing participants' diversity by getting to know about their proficiencies, using criteria to recognize the most important influences on their participation, using multiple sources to estimate relevant participant expectations, and using effective learning activities to enhance responsiveness.

This chapter provides a rationale for leaders' use of responsive methods. After a brief statement of the leaders' task, an example from the helping professions is provided, followed by various examples related to participant aspirations, self-concepts, session leader's suggestions, enterprise expectations, and indicators of benefits. The chapter concludes with a summary of questions to encourage formulation of guidelines for a specific session.

Task: Share a rationale for the session leader's use of content and learning methods that are responsive to participants and relevant to their performance. **Example:** Several categories of stakeholders can contribute to the enhancement of professional development activities, including enterprise staff that focus on applicability to quality improvement, content experts regarding concepts and examples, and experienced teachers and trainers on active learning procedures. Such stakeholder contributions were especially helpful in the following example of a director of a volunteers mentoring volunteers program.

Some hospital administrators had discovered that an effective volunteer program is a cost-beneficial way to supplement the specialized contributions of their employed, typically overworked health professionals. An important leadership contribution of a nurse who was an able director of volunteers was to align specific and varied volunteer skills with the tasks they could perform for patients and staff.

Many volunteers have experience in the helping professions (such as nurses, teachers, clergy, and counselors), and some of them became volunteers because an acquaintance expressed great satisfaction from part-time interaction with appreciative patients.

To ensure the volunteer program served as a bonus and not an interference, several experienced volunteers assisted the director with mentoring and coordinating volunteer contributions with the hospital staff. Mentoring topics included patient education; reading; children's games; conversation; arranging flowers; communication; and, most important, teamwork with the health professionals and staff members.

Volunteers ranged in age from teens to retirees. In the past couple of decades the proportion of male volunteers has been increasing. A basic method of orienting and assisting volunteers was on-the-job training and peer mentoring. Because the participants were volunteers, methods were more informal and individualized than is the case for typical staff development. However, most of these volunteers responded well to typical professional learning sessions because of their high levels of motivation and relevant work experience.

This example illustrates a few ways the leader can guide a responsive session, such as focusing on performance, obtaining stakeholders' suggestions, encouraging self-selection, using mentoring, and using explicit criteria to select effective learning methods. However, each session reflects distinctive participant characteristics and the leader's style. The remainder of the chapter includes various examples and related rationales about useful concepts. Together, this overview of possibilities illustrates some of the different ways sessions can be responsive to participants and suggests a few ways to enhance responsiveness in specific instances.

A question for activity leaders to consider is, To what personal and performance features of participants should leaders be especially responsive? Session participants vary greatly in many characteristics; however, may be less diverse than for other types of educational activities for adults because of their professional preparation and occupational focus, as well as their choosing the session because of its content and convenience, such as cost and scheduling.

However, only a small number of personal and performance variations warrant major responsiveness by activity leaders. For significant participant characteristics, effective session leaders should refer to established explanations of these characteristics so they can get to know the participants and their activity and, therefore, be responsive to participants' characteristics and expectations.

Examples of personal characteristics to assess include participants' current proficiencies (combinations of knowledge, skills, and attitudes), change orientations, special abilities, communication style, and expectations of what will be gained from an activity. Examples of performance-related characteristics are participants' reflections on the extent and type of their work-related experience and roles and their ongoing connections with communities of practice.

Effective professional learning activity leaders understand that they, helpers, and resource people; actual session methods and opportunities; and the participants themselves can contribute to program responsiveness. The following examples illustrate why and how leaders can enhance responsiveness. These examples pertain to participant expectations, self-concept, leaders' suggestions, enterprise expectations, and indicators of benefits.

A member's decision to participate in a professional development activity usually reflects multiple motives and expectations. Sometimes familiarity with similar activities and leaders results in an excellent fit between participants' expectations and program objectives. This alignment can enhance learning and human potential in general. Such examples of effective leadership can suggest ways to strengthen planning and recruitment for future activities and thus increase the proportion of very satisfied participants.

Ongoing program evaluation can identify characteristics and participants' reasons why the session objectives and activities were less responsive to them. Evaluation results and feedback can indicate the necessity of modifying concepts and procedures to attract and select participants, modify activity objectives, and strengthen connections with organizations related to professional performance. Such refinements can help enhance professional performance and quality improvement. Increased alignment and responsiveness is doubly important because the greatest influence on newcomers is word-of-mouth recommendations from satisfied participants. Also, a beneficial activity experience increases the likelihood of participants' ongoing learning and progress.

Professional learning activity participants each have their own distinctive sense of self, which may reflect various levels of confidence, openness to change, preference for affiliation, and emphasis on achievement. Such preferences can connect with level of expertise, occupational role, contextual influences, and preferred learning styles. Experienced activity leaders who reflect on their impressions of participants from similar past sessions (based on introductions, interaction, evaluation feedback, simulation, performance, and informal conversations) can become increasingly alert to similarities and differences compared to current participants and thus modify programs accordingly to enhance responsiveness.

Activity leaders at any level of experience in conducting professional learning events can seek suggestions from various stakeholders, especially from very effective leaders. Such suggestions regarding planning, conducting, and evaluating professional learning can contribute to activity improvements in ways similar to those employed by experts in content or technology. Increasing use of technology to plan, conduct, record, and evaluate activities can make excellent examples of use by participants available to leaders who want to enhance their programs.

Participants' prior work experience can influence responsiveness in several ways. Examples of resistance to change can include participant restrictions on related time and expenditures and discouragement regarding applications of activity concepts to actual performance. Sometimes participants and their work associates will appreciate the benefits from participation that help explain why such participation tends to be cost beneficial.

By contrast, many enterprises (business, government, military, health, education, community agencies) have strong commitments to human resource development (staff development, training, professional development) with policies for released time from work and allocation of resources to support learning and quality improvement.

Various criteria are used as indicators of potential benefits that warrant investments and resources for professional learning, including certification of participation and achievement by accredited providers and assessment conclusions about increased quality and achievement by professionals, individually and in teams. In some fields, assessment includes indicators of benefits for recipients of professional services. For professionals in organizational settings, a 360-degree evaluation provides evidence from people in various roles who interact with a professional.

The following four elements are strategies to enhance responsiveness of leaders of professional learning activities: current proficiencies, interactions with peers, change orientation, and guidance from professional publications.

Current proficiencies. An assessment of a participant's current knowledge, skills, and attitudes related to professional learning activities is one of the most useful generalizations as a basis for conducting an effective program. The assessment conclusions can enable an effective leader to estimate readiness and relevance early in the activity and achievement of progress toward the end. Program responsiveness is enhanced along with participant engagement.

A leader who works closely with activity participants can use ongoing evaluation to assess shifting levels of proficiency related to major aspects of professional performance emphasized in a program. Sometimes an external evaluator is a valuable investment if objectivity regarding somewhat controversial issues is important. Assessment of unmet educational needs should include assessment by participants themselves and by one or more external assessments to estimate and address discrepancies that are between trivial and intimidating. Such cross-validation is important for learners and the people who help them learn.

Interactions with peers. Peer interaction may be encouraged when an activity leader seeks greater networking, formal feedback, and teamwork. Arrranging to have participants interact with resource people can increase relevance on specialized topics. Communities of practice depend on voluntary informal learning and mentoring, which session leaders can explain and encourage in ways similar to those of self-help groups and journal clubs. Sustained participation depends on motivation and volunteer leadership to enable professionals to enter and benefit from such networks.

Change orientation. In organizational settings, there tend to be three somewhat distinct psychological orientations to change that can lead to constructive interaction. Conservers prefer gradual changes in predictable work arrangements. Originators welcome innovation and opportunities to serve as change agents. Pragmatists are team-oriented practical mediators who prefer useful outcomes and problem solving.

Guidance from professional publications. Leaders can suggest relevant publications to encourage session members to engage in inquiry and innovation to achieve greater depth by casually mentioning a publication, distributing lists of readings, or providing a bibliographic essay. Session leaders can enhance responsiveness by suggesting electronic and print publications that allow participants to pursue specialized topics.

These concepts and examples about responsiveness to participants illustrate the importance of ongoing exploration of responsiveness, relevance to improved performance, focusing on important variations in experience and expectations, understanding multiple influences, sources of indicators, and using responsive learning activities.

The following questions are intended to encourage a leader to formulate a few guidelines for selection and use of methods that are aligned with the session's objectives, the leader's style, and the participants' characteristics:

1. How might an activity leader estimate the readiness of participants to enhance their professional performance?
2. How can participants' views of influences on performance in their workplace enable a leader to use responsive methods and concepts?
3. What are some efficient ways for leaders to understand a manageable number of participant characteristics, proficiencies, change orientations, and expectations to consider along with specific program goals?
4. On what types of criteria might a leader focus in order to be responsive to participants' organizational roles and expectations?
5. How can activity stakeholders and resource people suggest useful ways to increase responsiveness?
6. What contributions to responsiveness reflect communities of practice and professional publications? How can responsiveness to participants be enhanced by the use of technology, simulations, portfolios, and evaluation feedback to make connections between learning and performance?

4

SPECIFYING CURRENT PARTICIPANT PROFICIENCIES

An estimate of participants' current professional knowledge, skills, and attitudes related to activity goals is one of the most important understandings for a session leader to help participants learn. An effective leader can obtain relevant information and compose a useful estimate in various ways.

Activity leaders can gradually refine the estimates with assistance from participants, peers, and published standards. Leaders can enhance proficiencies by using case examples that include peer interactions. Portfolios can help participants build on multiple abilities with leaders supporting and challenging them. Ongoing evaluation feedback regarding enhanced proficiency can contribute to progress during and following a seminar.

After a brief statement of the leadership task, there is an example from the helping professions, followed by various pertinent concepts and some additional examples. The chapter concludes with suggested questions regarding selection of guidelines.

Task: Specify participants' current professional proficiencies as a foundation on which to build during learning activities.

Example: A research-oriented university established a teaching academy (TA) based on a proposal unanimously approved by the Faculty Senate. The initial slate of TA fellows included experienced faculty members who were well regarded for their teaching and scholarship. The TA fellows were responsible for creating detailed plans regarding mission and procedures, such as the annual selection of fellows for three-year renewable terms and guidelines for faculty development. Applicants and their colleagues submitted a statement about the applicants' expectations of how TA membership would enhance their teaching and that of their colleagues. Members of the selection committee read the applications and recommended new members for full membership.

Although a few accepted the honor but were largely inactive, most participated actively in monthly meetings, committees, and various faculty development activities for members and any other interested faculty. The TA was a freestanding unit with a graduate assistant (who had experience in professional development), meeting place, funding for communication, and responsibility to submit an annual report to the Faculty Senate.

The TA assessed members' current teaching proficiencies (knowledge, skills, attitudes) in various ways, including interactions with members of the self-governing unit, formulation of selection criteria for new members, and creation and participation in committees, for example, on evaluation of teaching, use of educational technology, innovative teaching and learning activities, and interaction with graduate students as teaching assistants. Some pairs of TA members exchanged observations and peer reviews of their teaching with very useful feedback.

Once or twice a year, the TA sponsored a daylong symposium on selected aspects of teaching excellence open to interested faculty and students. In each of these activities, participants helped make explicit and shared current and desired knowledge, skills, and attitudes that reflected typical teaching performance and exemplary teaching and learning that illustrated achievable standards of best practice, especially narratives of members' progress toward enhanced teaching. This faculty development activity was coordinated, planned, and conducted by the members, similar to a journal club. Members' current abilities were reflected in their active participation and results.

For any professional development activity, leaders can decide which features of participants' proficiencies are especially important to understand. Good estimates of current participant capabilities can guide other program decisions by a leader and other session planners. An estimate should be focused on current capabilities that are relevant to the objectives of professional development activities. Sometimes participants can point to an experience that they feel seems to prepare them to progress toward achieving the program objectives. Information from assessments about general proficiencies at the beginning and end of the activity, plus self-selection, can provide a good start.

Asking participants to introduce themselves, state their expectations for the activity, and mention relevant experience helps prepare the other participants and session leaders for possible adjustments. Leaders of well-planned learning events can select a sequence of goals and activities that fit participants' capabilities and expectations. Able leaders also understand that interactions among participants can enrich everyone's experience. Ongoing evaluation feedback and reflection also contribute to increased responsiveness to participants.

In the following example, an activity leader focused on the clinical practice in a surgical specialty:

> Participants were varied in their preparation and experience related to surgery. This diversity was reflected in the participants' interactions before and during each one-hour case conference session. Each week, a patient scheduled for surgery was selected as the subject for the case conference. During a few days before each weekly session, participants and staff reviewed the available information about the patient.
>
> Participants at various stages of clinical preparation focused on somewhat different aspects. During each activity, the sole focus was on what should be done for a patient. The participants made suggestions, and the staff asked inquiry clarification questions that promoted active information seeking. Available information regarding patient cases varied in the extent of information and evident procedures to follow.
>
> Some participants may have felt they had insufficient information for discussing what to do about the patient's case. The staff wanted to be supportive and responsive to participants with varied clinical experience, but they also wanted to challenge participants to become more analytical and self-directed in order to enhance their professional development.

In another example, participants were very diverse in their current proficiencies. Activity leaders evaluated participants' varied backgrounds, educational preparation, and work so they could use their conclusions to enrich the course, encourage peer exchange, and enhance learning among participants.

An easy way for a leader to be responsive to participant viewpoints and current levels of understanding is an audience response system in which each participant has an electronic clicker. Participants can quickly indicate their understanding or interest by anonymously clicking their preferences for answers, which allows the event leader immediately to assess attitudes about an activity topic or knowledge of major concepts. This form of evaluation feedback from participants enables a leader to immediately make adjustments and respond to participants' current proficiencies, reinforce their mastery, and guide their progress toward desired proficiencies and professional standards.

Proficiencies can be estimated in different ways when assisting only a small group of participants, such as mentoring young professionals to assess their own current proficiencies. In the following example, a primary care faculty member spent an hour with a few participants in the first of a series of sessions on a clinical topic:

> Group members met in a small conference room with a whiteboard, table, and chairs. This first meeting began with introductions and a brief overview of the activity topic.
>
> Using a blank chart for each participant, the leader wrote potential clinical decisions on the whiteboard and then asked participants to suggest likely uses in clinical practice by major stakeholders regarding either desired clinical procedures with decisions to be made or risks to be considered. This simulation enabled the participants to discuss the topic actively, and it allowed the leader to assess their current proficiency and decide how they would proceed during the remainder of the hour.
>
> The session had a conversational quality; brief questions and answers were interspersed with longer explanations that included references to additional personal and situational influences on the decision-making process, implications for alternative procedures, and various stakeholder perspectives. Participants seemed ready for the leader's detailed answers.

Activity leaders can assess features of participants' current proficiencies in various formal and informal ways, such as defining and evaluating proficiency; illustrating aspects of the topic related to the discussion's focus; and using conclusions about participants' proficiencies for session planning, improvement, and evaluation.

An adult's current proficiency includes a combination of knowledge, skills, and attitudes that constitute his or her capability to perform well if given an opportunity. This distinction is important because many educational and training activities emphasize only knowledge gained, although improved performance also entails changes in skills and attitudes.

The following are some of the many proficiency assessment procedures available to activity leaders:

1. Encourage participants to engage in self-assessment and obtain an assessment from an additional source.
2. Evaluate proficiency based on recent information about participants' educational preparation and experience.

3. Provide opportunities for participants to engage in peer review.
4. Assist participants in assembling a narrative or portfolio of their career progress.
5. Arrange for participants to engage in a community of practice, which might clarify for everyone the participant's current proficiency.
6. Prepare participants to complete an examination associated with career advancement.
7. Discuss professional standards and guidelines for practice and ways to reflect on the implications for current proficiency.
8. Use feedback from an ongoing evaluation to clarify current proficiency.

Leaders and interested participants can use proficiency evaluations in various ways for planning, improving, and assessing professional development. A basic method is to use a sound estimate of a participant's current knowledge, skills, and attitudes related to activity objectives as a foundation for a combination of supportive and challenging learning activities. This understanding can prompt participants to raise growth-inducing questions and leaders to provide answers that lead to further growth.

As a series of sessions progresses, conclusions from assessments of current proficiencies can be used to guide the learning process and gradually modify learning activities and reinforce increasing levels of mastery. Leaders can also use conclusions regarding current proficiency for assisting with self-assessments; guiding decision-making practice by use of actual, virtual, or speculative examples; and developing simulations, which enable participants to model, assess, and enhance professional practice. Additional uses of estimates of participants' current proficiencies include guiding learning activities and reflecting on seminar results, portfolios, exams, mentoring and coaching, and computer-related achievement trends.

These concepts and examples on specifying current proficiencies illustrate activities that leaders can use as proficiency evaluations for planning simulations and other learning activities to build multiple abilities.

The following questions are intended to encourage your reflection on the process of specifying session participants' current proficiencies:

1. For previous programs, in what ways did you estimate participants' current proficiencies, such as self-assessment, prior experience, peer review, standards, and evaluation feedback?
2. How might guidelines related to current proficiencies help you contribute to assisting with self-assessments; encourage commitment to change, use of examples, and use of simulations; and reinforce increasing levels of mastery?

3. How might conclusions from specifying participants' current proficiencies enhance your focus on improved performance and provide supportive and challenging learning activities?
4. Which proficiency assessment procedures would you like to emphasize more in future activities?

5

DEVELOPING SHARED EXPECTATIONS

ffective professional development activity leaders, planners, and participants use shared explanations of desired participant proficiencies to guide participants' progress during and following a session. This chapter provides ways the leader can obtain and use shared expectations of stakeholders to guide planning and conducting a session.

Activities can be enhanced when leaders and participants have similar expectations about the types of desired proficiencies participants seek, along with timing during an activity, and ways to achieve them. Estimates of proficiencies can be provided and shared by participants, leaders, and other stakeholders, including observers. Shared explanations about expectations can be contributed and used by participants, leaders, and other stakeholders.

After a brief statement of the leadership task, there is an example from the helping professions, followed by various pertinent concepts and some additional examples. The chapter concludes with suggested questions regarding selection of guidelines.

Task: Formulate preliminary explanations of desired participant proficiencies as expressed before and during the session by leaders, planners, and participants to contribute to achievement of shared learning purposes.

Example: A professional association's director of professional development was aware that concurrent sessions during association conferences were variably successful in actually increasing members' technical performance. The director decided to invite members who were consistently excellent presenters to lead a demonstration session and allow an expert on teaching and learning to observe each concurrent session and prepare summaries of the teaching and learning concepts that were demonstrated.

41

The summaries did not include the specific content and identity of the leaders and participants; after activity leaders reviewed the drafts, they were shared with other potential presenters to illustrate concepts and procedures they might consider to enhance their educational effectiveness. Each summary included ways leaders and participants stated their expectations and provided ongoing evaluation feedback about participants' progress. Several dozen such summaries of observations and interviews regarding teaching concepts and methods were prepared for similar professional fields so that the summaries were useful for various presenters.

Because activity leaders varied in teaching style, session objectives, and numbers and characteristics of participants, summaries selected by people who wanted to improve their programs illustrated a few promising innovations. As activity leaders reviewed summaries, reflected on implications for their sessions regarding making teacher and participant expectations explicit, considered evaluation feedback from participants, and discussed feedback with a few other leaders, they tended to internalize useful methods that gradually became part of their usual teaching style. Activity participants and leaders can improve their sessions by obtaining estimates of expectations from participants, peers, and observers for the purposes of planning and ongoing progress.

Activity leaders should consider why and how stakeholders might understand participants' desired proficiency. Members' decisions to participate in a professional development activity typically reflect multiple motives and reasons. Their expressed expectations for an activity indicate some of the reasons, which are usually associated with enhanced performance or quality improvement. Other motives for some participants may have little to do with enhanced mastery and benefits but pertain more to fellowship, location, respite, or professional requirement.

Some early session activities can clarify participants' motives and guide program decisions of leaders and participants, for example, using participant expectations to shape activity topics; reflecting on simulations to reveal connections between session content and personal applications; providing ongoing evaluation feedback to align activities with participant expectations; or allowing participants to select from optional activities, which is an unobtrusive way for a leader to discover participant expectations. Asking participants to map their perceived connections among expectations and session goals, career directions and professional goals, and the combination of personal and situational influences on their performance and quality of practice can deepen some members' understanding of career priorities. Making such connections explicit can stimulate reflection on priorities.

The following example illustrates some of the ways an activity leader can address participant expectations:

An activity leader explained how and why a procedure, which was the focus of a three-hour session, was initially used. The leader's goal was to provide a historical overview of the influences and early criticism as well as the growing use of the procedure, evolving evidence, and increasing acceptance and amount of use. The leader's style was informal and interactive. Highlights of an article by a highly respected member of the profession recognized various views on the advantages and disadvantages of the procedure. The participants were encouraged to ask questions about the rationale for using and documenting the procedure. Visuals showing excellent results with well know and less well known people were provided along with the leader's views on persistence, excellence, appearances, diversity, resistance, perception, and responsiveness from the perspective of the professionals and the people they serve.

After a few comments and visuals, a series of steps, and a caution about a difficult procedure, participants asked two dozen questions in a short time. The next segment was very interactive and included using valuable questions from experienced participants to clarify procedures for the less experienced, asking participants to identify potential options, referring to research evidence, providing elaboration on an earlier answer, summarizing some basic points that had been discussed, and appreciating the value of challenging procedures and differing views because that's how people learn.

The final hour was about joint decisions by a member of the profession and the person being served. A review of professional procedures was given by the leader, interspersed with humorous comments, mild self-criticism, research evidence, and suggested future readings. The iterative process during this concurrent session was described as successive approximations in which the results of early stages help shape options and procedures for subsequent stages.

Finally, the leader reviewed the main concepts and emphasized recognition of the growing edge of change and learning in the profession, welcomed the challenges of innovation and excellence, and expressed appreciation to the participants for their conversation during the session.

What features late in the session were likely to make explicit some of the expectations that were shared by participants and the activity leader? What might the leader have done additionally to increase agreement and cooperation as the session unfolded?

It is not easy for activity leaders, participants, and coordinators to quickly assess participants' desired knowledge, skills, and attitudes related to program objectives and content. Fortunately, leaders can select and assemble conclusions from various sources of information as an estimate of what participants want to gain from the activity and use to improve their performance. In addition, including participants and the coordinator in assembling this estimate contributes to using it for session planning and improvement. If the activity leader and coordinator provide ongoing evaluation feedback to stakeholders, conclusions about desired proficiencies constitute an early stage of ongoing evaluation.

The main sources of information are the participants, the leader, and session activities. The leader should note participants' words and actions. If additional stakeholders such as the coordinator and helpers attend sessions, they can assist the leader with making brief notes. Information about participant expectations may be reviewed and summarized to guide activity planning and improvement, in part by sharing conclusions with participants.

The leader can then select the types of information about expectations to focus on, which simplifies the process. The leader's program planning can include the aspects of desired proficiencies to guide plans and decisions for which the leader is the main source. Such information for planning can reflect the leader's words, session activities, and resources and may be of interest regarding ongoing professional development.

Information about activities and external resources can be integral to conducting the session and just have to be noted and included in the process of decision making. Based on the foregoing examples regarding participant expectations, leaders can select from among various indicators that are most relevant to the activity's purpose and participant characteristics. Including at least one piece of information from each can increase cross-validation for useful estimates.

Two ways participants indicate program-related proficiencies they hope to gain are *participants' comments* about such expectations and their implicit *choices* during a session. The leader can demonstrate to participants a commitment to explicit reflection about intentions in order to improve a relevant aspect of performance. Thus, a participant's words and choices constitute the first and second category of indicators.

Three additional indicators are the *leader's comments* about alignment of participant reasons for participation and session objectives; the leader's inclusion of session *activities* related to this alignment; and, finally, the leader's *encouragement* of participants to pursue learning resources related to the program's purpose beyond the session activities.

This component of guiding professional development is intended to estimate efficiently collective participant expectations to enhance their proficiencies specifically related to session objectives. Such estimates by the leader, to plan and assess the activity, should be modified as the session progresses. It is not intended to provide a more rigorous assessment of individual participant professional proficiency in general.

The following examples are based on participant comments about the reasons for pursuing session objectives. Before or during an activity, participants may introduce or describe their career or reason for participation by expressing what they want to gain from the session. Because collective preferences (other than unusual individual expectations) tend to guide program decisions, inclusions of representative participants' preferences are combined with expectations of other stakeholders. This agreement constitutes shared expectations.

Another indicator of expressed expectations is participant feedback to the session leader. An additional indicator is the distribution of participant preferences among the available options for subgroup goals, content, or activities. Participants' comments on their perceived connections between their past professional experiences in preparation for future progress are an additional indicator. Another is participants' explanations about why and how they are progressing, and another could be reflected in participants' comments on career goals. A further indicator could be part of participants' broad rationale for their career, including values, goals, and activities along with personal and situational influences.

The following are additional examples of expectations based on participant choices. One such indicator is based on observations of participants' choices among optional areas of proficiency. Another is based on observation of voluntary peer interactions related to the various areas of proficiency to be developed. Participants' seeking information related to proficiency areas provides an additional indicator; another is implicit motives for seeking to achieve session objectives. A further indicator is observations about participant persistence related to proficiencies and program objectives and activities.

The remaining leader-based indicators are the leader's guidelines, observations, and suggestions. One indicator is the leader's comments about professional excellence and how to achieve it. An indicator can be included in leader feedback regarding participant progress. Another type is leader feedback to participants about their plans to enhance their proficiencies and general performance. A leader's comment on excellence as a criterion for his or her session activities is an additional indicator. Another is encouragement of participants to be analytical, reflective, and self-directed in the pursuit of learning activity goals.

Other sources of leader-based indicators are parts of the program structure leaders include to guide participant progress toward achievement of activity goals, one of which is provision of illustrative innovations by members of the profession, and another is explanations about excellent performance. Additional indicators are stakeholder agreement on activity goals, analyses of examples, and simulations that help participants prepare, practice, obtain feedback. Another is understanding how things work in aspects of professional performance related to program goals. Additional indicators result from stakeholder agreement on activity goals, making session objectives explicit, the iterative process of goal-setting activities, and evaluation feedback regarding progress (such as modification of goals and activities).

Activity planning can benefit from explicit indicators of progress. Leaders sometimes seek to guide participant growth and goal achievement regarding leader-initiated indicators. An indicator may result from leaders of similar sessions discussing how and why they help participants pursue expectations related to program goals. Another indicator results from feedback to the leader from observers of sessions that may lead to improvements. A leader-initiated indicator occurs when leaders encourage participants to consult research evidence, published articles, and documentation to pursue enhanced performance related to activity objectives. An additional leader-initiated indicator results from learner explanations of innovative trends in the professional field that may inspire participants to pursue session goals.

Effective leaders can encourage participant pursuit of excellence by assembling outstanding examples for activity stakeholders to assess. Ongoing evaluation can guide the identification of stakeholders and suggest ways in which they can assist. Scholars, knowledge brokers, interested participants, and other people can engage in inquiry and reflection to specify multiple sources of conclusions from research and professional practice that can inform standards of achievable best practice relevant to program objectives.

Journalists, educators, and writers can use presentations, media, and publications to raise the consciousness of professionals, people in related occupations, and the general public regarding the sources, importance, and implications of professional learning and action objectives based on evidence-informed standards.

Active inclusion of program participants and their peers in reflection and action regarding such objectives can inspire increased mastery and improved professional performance during and beyond professional development activities. Session leaders can increase the extent and effectiveness of such follow-through by giving explicit attention during activities to their rationale and procedures for ongoing inquiry, self-reflection, and feedback by participants as part of their professional performance following the learning activity.

The following overview reviews ways session leaders can effectively estimate participants' collective expectations to progress toward their desired proficiencies, aligned with session objectives. This can enable activity leaders to review these indicators, decide which ones they already use, modify their ways of estimating participant expectations, and use the resulting conclusions to increase session effectiveness.

Able session leaders can help gain agreement on high-priority participant expectations that fit session goals, along with efficient ways to estimate and use shared expectations to guide ongoing learning and performance improvement.

Your reflections on the following questions regarding shared expectations can lead to guidelines for your specific session:

1. How might you increase the effectiveness and efficiency of guiding participants' comments about their expectations for an activity?
2. How might you also note instances in which participants make changes early in the session that reflect their commitment to improve an aspect of performance that is relevant to activity goals?
3. How might you better align and modify the fit of shared participant expectations with session goals, activities, and resources?
4. How might you enhance your efforts to increase alignment by offering comments on excellence, providing feedback to participants on their plans and progress, giving attention to organizational initiatives, referring them to standards, and enhancing participants' self-directed learning?
5. How might you organize activities regarding progress toward stakeholder agreement on goals, explicit goals, excellent performance, and use of examples?
6. How might you enrich your understanding of participant expectations by consultation with other session leaders; feedback from observations of the activity; encouragement of participants' use of research, publications, and documentation; and explanations of innovation and trends?

6

ADDRESSING GAPS
BETWEEN CURRENT AND
DESIRED PROFICIENCIES

Along with estimating participants' current abilities and expectations related to activity goals, a major leadership task is to help participants narrow the gap (discrepancy) between their current and desired proficiencies. Effective leaders efficiently assess such gaps to help achieve activity goals through attention to estimates of gaps, influences on proficiencies, activities, and outcomes. Suggested ways to obtain and use such estimates are presented in this chapter.

Leaders can help participants at successive program stages regarding understanding of discrepancies related to participant and session goals, persisting in relevant practice to enhance proficiency, understanding multiple influences on learning and proficiency, using various ways to assess discrepancies, engaging in activities to reduce gaps, using feedback, and being reflective about their professional learning expectations and progress.

After a brief statement of the leadership task, there is an example from the helping professions, followed by various pertinent concepts and some additional examples. The chapter concludes with suggested questions regarding selection of guidelines.

Task: Discuss with activity stakeholders the evolving gaps between participants' current and desired proficiencies and consider how to narrow them.

Example: Reducing discrepancies is sometimes the major focus of professional learning activities. For various reasons and periods of time, such as full-time teaching appointments or positions in administration, some members of health professions depart from active clinical practice in midcareer to participate in their own professional development activities. Some universities and associations have contributed to midcareer professional learning activities to enable older members to renew their licensure/registration/certification so they can resume their clinical practice.

A major responsibility of the leader of this type of learning opportunity in one state was to inform interested members of the profession of their major gaps between current and desired proficiencies and then to assist each member in designing an individualized series of activities to achieve relicensure and resume clinical practice. Some assessment and enhancement procedures that help document current and desired proficiencies include specialty exams and simulations, mentoring, observations, interviews, peer review, and self-assessment. Carefully selected multiple assessment procedures can contribute to validity, participant motivation, efficiency, and high-quality performance. The leader of this relicensure opportunity discovered that useful modules, procedures, mentors, and examples had accumulated and could be selected and modified for efficient use with similar members interested in relicensure.

The foregoing example includes sources of estimates about discrepancies such as observations, interviews, peer reviews, and simulations. The next example contains some additional sources and uses of estimates, such as shared objectives, group discussion, reflection on priority activities, and feedback from ongoing evaluation.

As you review the following example, note the features that are most pertinent to reducing discrepancies between current and desired capabilities. The example illustrates various ways to help participants in any professional field recognize discrepancies between desirable standards and their current mastery of proficiencies.

This workshop leader had a stage presence characterized by clear and interesting explanations, humor, and responsiveness to helpers and participants. The leader introduced the session with a PowerPoint slide that listed three workshop objectives. The introduction also stressed the importance of mastering content from the workshop to use later and asked participants about their expectations for the session. After initial expectations were expressed by participants, the leader asked for others and received a dozen more. This was followed by a series of PowerPoint slides, each of which focused on major concepts of excellence, including a list of key phrases. The concepts included the criteria of excellence, high success rates, increased chances of success, and the importance of ongoing evaluation contributing to improved professional performance.

The leader noted the importance of professional judgment when there was a lack of research evidence to guide some decisions, referred to a research report applicable to a decision, and encouraged participants to follow the advice of mentors. The leader then showed a series of slides on risk and decision making and used models and graphic displays to generate proposed solutions. About 20 minutes into the session, the leader provided background information about a case example, explained the stages of decision making, showed results, and encouraged participants to work with other team members.

The next example suggests more ways to clarify discrepancies, such as using simulations, standards, publications, and plans. Following this example is an overview of concepts and procedures a leader can use to help participants narrow gaps related to session goals.

About 30 minutes into the session, the leader provided a step-by-step demonstration using a visualizer (overhead projector and a large screen) so that everyone could see details, followed by questions and answers. Going through some simulations allowed participants opportunities to try, receive feedback, and reflect on the process of gradual mastery. As part of the second simulation, the leader used the visualizer to demonstrate additional details and processes. The leader noted that excellent performance includes knowledge, skills, and attitudes, and then used several slides to illustrate the use of professional judgment to explain professional considerations while respecting the judgments of the people participants serve.

Toward the end of the session, the leader discussed critical thinking by various stakeholders in which a professional weighs positive and negative views as a way of arriving at results that are mutually satisfactory for the professional and the client. Many questions and answers followed on topics such as using standards of excellence to guide progress, team member contributions, cautions related to timing of performance improvement efforts, and a participant's suggestion regarding discussing progress to achieve feedback and reinforce gradual improvement. The leader's commentary included tips and ways to increase chances for success, citations of articles for later reading (on selection of procedures to produce the best results), and explanations about workshop materials participants might find helpful.

Later in the activity, the leader mentioned some trends over the years that reflected improvements in typical performance. During this segment, the leader used explanations, demonstrations, participant practice, and feedback in response to participants' questions and results. This included use of models for simulation by the teacher and participants, accompanied by guidelines participants could use for plans, decisions, and actions at the workshop session and at work.

A helper made an additional comment, and the leader noted the upcoming shift to the next stage of the workshop, answered a question, and passed around an example prepared beforehand that illustrated the procedure that was just reviewed. The leader next used several slides to illustrate the use of professional judgment to explain considerations when there is no clear guideline while respecting the judgments of the people professionals serve. Many questions and answers followed on topics such as using standards of excellence to guide progress, occasional corrections, team member contributions, and a caution related to timing.

Effective activity leaders efficiently estimate evolving gaps between participants' current and desired proficiencies. Such estimates contribute to developing activity goals and deciding how to gradually narrow the changing gap between educational needs and mastery during and beyond the session. Indicators of discrepancies the activity leader can use for such estimates are similar and in addition to the separate indicators of current and desired proficiencies.

It is important to focus on discrepancies in addition to expectations because the gaps gradually evolve over the years as members improve their current mastery while progress in the professional field can raise the bar of achievable standards of best practice. Activity stakeholders vary in their perceptions of discrepancies. Estimates that reflect varied perceptions of gaps by participants and coordinators as well as session leaders are especially valuable because each person can contribute to narrowing the discrepancies. The following is an overview of indicators of discrepancies: estimates, influences, activities, and outcomes.

Estimates. Effective session leaders efficiently estimate evolving gaps between participants' current and desired proficiencies. Use of such indicators can guide decisions for activity planning, improvement, and assessment. Selected indicators should pertain to current discrepancies related to session objectives and ongoing professional development goals. Potential assessment procedures include self-assessments, observations, questions and answers, interviews, peer reviews, exams, and simulations. Leaders can also estimate participant abilities (such as memory, inquiry, and learning style) that are likely to influence progress.

Influences. The following are some of the many potential influences on efforts to narrow discrepancies, a few of which can provide estimates leaders can use to guide session activities:

1. Participants' perceptions and expectations about feelings of empathy related to activity objectives
2. Agreement on explicit, clear, and realistic learning objectives that can help participants understand the gaps
3. Guidelines and criteria regarding standards of excellence and quality that can help focus on especially important discrepancies

4. Feedback from ongoing evaluation that can guide gradual narrowing of such gaps
5. Contributions by mentors whose precept and example can reinforce personal resolve and efforts to narrow gaps
6. Reflection by participants regarding their past performance successes and their views about likely future performance quality
7. Evidence of team contributions to professional performance and growth
8. Contributions of research and other publications that can focus on important discrepancies to be reduced
9. Awareness of trends and influences of the professional field pertinent to important evolving discrepancies
10. Participant change events that can trigger heightened readiness to learn related to such gaps

Activities. To focus on narrowing gaps, leaders can emphasize some of the following activities related to session goals and participant receptivity: evaluation feedback, questions, demonstrations, case examples and simulations, explanations, practice related to narrowing the gap, reflection, innovation, inquiry, and discovery. Other stakeholders can assist with planning and conducting such activities to reduce discrepancies.

Outcomes. Leader and participant interactions to narrow gaps can strengthen the path to achieve desirable outcomes during and following professional learning activities. The first contribution is understanding that effective practice can modify mental, physical, and attitudinal capacity throughout one's professional career. The second contribution is recognition that participants usually have multiple abilities regarding narrowing gaps related to various proficiencies. The third contribution is appreciation of the extent to which able professionals transcend their focus on their own career to embrace valuable connections with peers, members of related occupations, and the people they serve. The fourth contribution is participant aging and reflection on influences, assumptions, and intentions that affect professional performance, including enhancing current proficiencies and expanding desired proficiency. The fifth contribution is use of creativity to deepen and expand professional roles and practice. The sixth contribution is consideration of the contributions of metacognition related to decision making, analysis, critical thinking, judgment, and wisdom.

Leaders can help participants experience activities and related feedback that enable them to progress toward improved performance during and following professional development sessions. Facilitation of participants' reduction of such discrepancies can be guided when leaders share concepts and implications through procedures such as estimating discrepancies, focusing on relevant program objectives, including active participant decision making, providing feedback with realistic examples, and using participants' enhanced proficiency for continuous improvement of professional performance.

The concepts and examples about how leaders can guide narrowing the evolving gap between current and desired proficiencies include understanding discrepancies, using practice for improved performance, recognizing influences, selecting forms of assessment, benefiting from pertinent learning activities, and reflecting on gradual occupational mastery.

These examples and concepts about reducing discrepancies between current mastery and desired proficiencies related to activity goals suggest many possibilities. As you review the following questions about estimates of discrepancies, consider which ones suggest initiatives you want to explore as guidelines for your specific session:

1. What types of assessment procedures seem to be most appropriate for you, such as self-assessments, observations, discussions, interviews, peer reviews, exams, or simulations?

2. Which influences on discrepancies seem to be most relevant to a specific session, such as expectations, standards, mentors, teamwork, and publications?

3. Which session activities might be most beneficial regarding participant receptivity to narrowing gaps related to program goals such as questions, demonstrations, examples, evaluations, and reflections?

4. How might interactions with participants guide their achievement of activity objectives, such as practice, ability, peer interaction, reflection, creativity, and metacognition?

5. To what extent are research-to-practice guidelines relevant, appropriate, applicable, timely, and reasonable? (If they are not, how might such guidelines be improved?)

7

ANALYZING SITUATIONAL INFLUENCES ON PERFORMANCE

Professional performance is influenced by various situational features. Effective leaders analyze contextual influences to identify which to address with participants in order to guide their professional learning efforts. Potential influences on performance include role relationships, developments likely to affect performance, related organizations connected with professional performance, and quality improvement.

Session leaders can guide participants to understand situational influences on their professional performance in several ways. The first way is to help participants understand the complex interplay of personal and situational influences on their performance. The second way is to assist participants in analyzing external workplace influences (including regulations and standards) and in focusing on the most relevant influences. Third, activity leaders and participants can explore ways participants can assess, understand, and connect with various organizations, agencies, and groups through mutually beneficial cooperation. Fourth, they can use quality improvement, technology, and evaluation feedback to focus on major situational opportunities and threats related to important aspects of interprofessional learning and performance. Force-field analysis of the combination of supportive and resistance influences can help people diagnose an example.

After a brief statement of the leadership task, there is an example from the helping professions, followed by various pertinent concepts and some additional examples. The chapter concludes with suggested questions regarding selection of guidelines.

Task: Enable participants to analyze situational features that influence professional performance.

Example: Organizational collaboration can reveal some influences on performance. A family medicine clinic's purpose and mission included partnerships with neighborhood organizations to promote prevention and wellness. A public health nurse served as clinical leader for community outreach and interprofessional cooperation. The leader and several health coaches explored many mutually beneficial connections between the clinic and community organizations such as schools, enterprises, labor unions, faith communities, YMCAs and YWCAs, health clubs, environmental groups, community education groups, the county public health department, libraries, and regional planning groups. The role of the outreach leader and some health coaches included interaction with health professionals and staff engaged in health care for sick or injured patients, which is the main function of the clinic. They developed these partnerships for the sake of continuity of care, patient education, and potential cooperation for outreach prevention activities.

Every month or so, the outreach leader or one of the coaches interacted with one or more of the contact people from some of the community organizations, and this facilitated an exchange of ideas about health-related problems and opportunities that would be mutually beneficial. They recognized that informal interaction could lead to trust and then to more formal cooperation.

A desirable outcome of these many interactions was a subtly gradual recognition that community initiatives regarding wellness and illness could lead to forms of assistance valued by clinic staff and members of community organizations. This exchange contributed to the gradual evolution and sustainability of the outreach relationship.

Which features of collaboration in this example are likely influences on professional and participant performance? What additional information about influences might be obtained?

This example suggests a linkage role for an activity leader or associates who interact with people in the service area to seek increased cooperation. The essence of such an outreach role for mutually beneficial cooperation is sufficient connections with people from the organization that provide professional development activities and with people in the area who might benefit from professional performance. As a leader negotiates an exchange arrangement, this proactive effort can help identify and harness specific situational influences on current professional performance. Examples of local situational influences on performance include role relationships for potential session participants, major trends and developments that affect occupational performance, and other organizations in the service area likely to help or hinder professional performance. Interorganizational connections established during an exploratory stage can provide the basis for longer-term networking and cooperation. The resulting trusted teamwork can help identify situational influences that might lead to longer-term developments. How might such an activity leader analyze situational influences? One question for session leaders is, Which situational influences on professional learning and performance deserve special attention? The scope of professional development activities should include improvements in procedures participants use in their work and their understanding of broader organizational and societal influences on performance on themselves, their work associates, and the people they serve.

Three broad situational influences have high priority. One influence is the provision of professional learning and quality improvement opportunities by enterprises, educational institutions, and associations. Awareness of and participation in such opportunities can accelerate awareness of and efforts regarding excellent performance and quality improvement. People who do not know about situational influences are likely to emphasize procedural topics and dismiss questions that ask why. Participation in interprofessional education can help participants reflect on collaboration and policy influences. A second influence is societal trends and issues such as computer technology, which can affect work performance and professional learning. A third influence is organizational norms and expectations that can either help or hinder the related priority of quality improvement.

The next example focuses on multiple influences on professional performance. An interprofessional conference role-play simulation on issues specific to a given field can dramatically increase awareness among practitioners in related occupations about the value of interprofessional cooperation when practitioners are unaware of relevant information about field-specific topics that is known by practitioners in other occupations. Participants worked in the related occupational fields of education, health, law enforcement, social work, and criminal justice. The following summary of the half-day simulation illustrates the use of simulations in various professional fields:

> Following a typical morning conference session, an interprofessional team presented a well-planned simulation, prepared during the previous year, that took up the entire afternoon session. The activity began with a brief explanation of the simulation, after which participants and the session leaders met together throughout the afternoon at tables in teams of eight people for the case discussion. During each of the 12 stages of the simulation, a moderator explained the purposes, procedures, and starting and

ending times of the stage under discussion. Participants received additional information from members at other tables who had had experience that could be useful for the simulation.

During the 10-minute discussions in each of the 12 stages of the simulation, participants at each table discussed preliminary information about the case, shared their views and analyses of the case example, designated a group member to seek additional information from another table, began interpreting what they knew to explain the emerging narrative, and compared the simulated case narrative with their actual past experience in such situations. Several practitioners then shared their analysis of what others in various occupations were likely to have done in similar circumstances. Then the narrator and other simulation planners guided the total group discussion of insights gained and suggested guidelines for future practice. In their closing reflections on the conference feedback form, many participants expressed appreciation for new understandings and the implications for future interprofessional cooperation.

There are various ways activity leaders can decide on which situational influences on performance and learning to focus. One is to find out from potential and current participants which influences they are aware of and how those influences seem to affect their performance and their professional learning. After beginning with a shared perception of such influences, leaders and participants can gradually expand and refine their understanding and specify implications. Another focus is occupational procedures, using trends, influences, and implications for analysis.

A broader analysis can include organizational influences such as mission, structure, norms, and expectations. Quality improvement guidelines in some enterprises can reveal such organizational influences on performance quality, with direct relevance to member roles and contributions. Activity leaders and resource people who have experience with various organizations can recognize broader societal influences, including opportunities and threats related to professional performance. Conclusions from evaluation feedback can enable activity participants to reflect on many types of influences on their performance that can guide professional learning and activities.

Aside from ways to understand some broad influences on performance, professional learning activities can be designed to deepen understanding of specific influences. The earlier interprofessional simulation illustrates how a role-play simulation can unfold and help participants to better understand how and why interprofessional cooperation is important. Activity leaders typically benefit from assistance in planning and conducting low-technology simulations such as role playing and, especially, computer-based simulations. Such assistance can include team members with expertise regarding content, learning, and design. Criteria for effective simulations that deal with experiential learning and important influences include sufficient appeal to initiate and sustain engagement, adequate fidelity to the content standards of professional performance, and a spirit of inquiry that contributes to discovery throughout the learning process.

The foregoing concepts and examples regarding ways activity leaders can guide participants' attention to situational influences on performance include understanding complex influences on their performance, focusing on the most relevant influences, using mutually beneficial cooperation with related organizations, and exploring inquiry to focus on perceived opportunities and threats related to their learning about their professional performance.

The following questions should prompt your reflections about guidelines on sources and the results of such influences for your specific activity:

1. How might participants explain major external and organizational influences on their performance as a basis for discussing ways to address them?
2. How can an analysis of occupational procedures, trends, and quality improvement conclusions contribute to guidelines for a specific activity that seeks to explore influences on performance?
3. How should interactions among participants, leaders, and resource people yield additional guidelines regarding influences on performance that could contribute to an enhanced analysis for a specific session?
4. What pertinent conclusions from ongoing evaluation can be obtained that will help participants discuss situational influences?

PART THREE

ENHANCING DESIRED PERFORMANCE OF DIVERSE PARTICIPANTS

Regarding the connection in chapters 8 through 10 on enhancing the desired performance of diverse participants: The tasks in these chapters focus on a sequence of transactions among leaders and diverse participants by using relevant content and active learning methods that result in ongoing enhanced performance.

8

ENHANCING THE LEARNING TRANSACTION

Many leaders of professional development activities recognize that transactions among leaders and participants are the crucial component of each session. Most of the other components are secondary and contribute to planning and conducting active learning sessions. The examples and concepts in this chapter guide decisions by activity coordinators, leaders, and participants as they interact to achieve improved professional performance.

Transactions among activity participants and coordinators are central to creative professional learning. For excellent sessions, leaders and coordinators usually seek active engagement by participants (and some other stakeholders) in selected activities and related practice toward achieving shared objectives and evaluation feedback. Effective activity leaders guide exchanges for individuals, groups, and organizations by using guidelines to select from the options available on learning activities (mentoring, peer interaction, reading, technology-assisted learning, simulation) that enrich learning and improve performance during and following sessions. Quality indicators can undergird excellent leaders who stimulate participants' expectations, guide progress, and provide ongoing feedback.

After a brief statement of the leadership task, there is an example from the helping professions, followed by various pertinent concepts and some additional examples. The chapter concludes with suggested questions regarding selection of guidelines.

Task: Reflect on the process and outcomes of interactions among professional learning session leaders and participants.

Example: Transactions among leaders and participants can be face-to-face or mediated by print or electronic means or by exhibits. A consulting firm that had conducted a leadership development program for museum directors for years obtained a foundation grant for a similar program for museum educators associated with art, history, and science museums. These educators, who sometimes attended conferences of the National Association for Museum Directors and read its publications, welcomed the opportunity to interact and learn from their counterparts at museums of various sizes, collections, and regions. After two national programs were conducted in different regions, an evaluation report was prepared to aid planning, improving, and assessing the results for future professional learning activities for museum educators.

The report summary contained the following description of transactions between leaders and participants: Interested potential participants submitted a detailed proposal, including their past experience, current role, plan for improving some aspect of educational activities in their museum, and a letter from their museum director expressing support for the educator to attend the program and conduct an improvement project in his or her museum. Applicants who were selected as participants received an agenda and related information for a weeklong residential program along with readings suggested by members of the advisory committee. During the week, participants interacted in plenary and subgroup discussion sessions that reflected a size and type of museum. These learning activities were especially valuable for some participants who lacked contact with other museum educators, and they also participated in individualized sessions with program faculty and other participants. Participants continued to modify their proposed plan for museum education in their organization.

During the following three months, as participants implemented their plans, they interacted with other participants and mentors and attended a weekend reunion during which they shared the story of their improvement project and their future plans. The improvement action learning project provided an ongoing focus for each participant, enriched by interaction with peers, session leaders, and materials. Ongoing evaluation feedback contributed to an exchange of ideas, networking, and strategies for organizational change in their museums. Concurrent sessions and discussion groups by size and type of museum were especially valuable for those participants who lacked ongoing contact with museum educators elsewhere.

This initial example refers to several concepts, such as encouraging peer interaction to enhance active learning and application of learning, and guiding individualization of participant learning activities. The next example contains some additional concepts, such as helping participants address situational and personal influences that pertain to their ongoing professional development and assessing benefits to the provider organization that is planning and conducting the professional learning activities.

This example from another professional field was provided by a leader who served as coordinator of a professional development conference for a university health professions specialty department.

> The purpose of the conference was to have an expert related to the specialty interact with the participants to enable them to understand closely related content and procedures, including decisions about how and why to obtain diagnostic information, relations with patient care, and reimbursement procedures. This coordinator worked most closely with a faculty member from the specialty department who served as the conference faculty director. For this coordinator, who was new to the role, participation in a one-day conference served to increase personal visibility as well as the department's.
>
> The conference faculty director served as the core of the planning committee. The coordinator and the more prominent conference faculty director began their planning months before the one-day conference. Their decisions regarding conference objectives, content, and procedures were influenced by their understanding of influences on professional practice and the relationships between the specialty and the participants' primary care clinical practice. The coordinator arranged for interactions with multiple stakeholders for planning, conducting, and evaluating the one-day conference.
>
> Teamwork with the department faculty conference director was especially important for identifying and encouraging specialty department faculty members to conduct specific segments of the conference. They understood that their effective contributions to the conference could enhance departmental visibility by participants' referring patients to the department and related hospitals and clinics. The coordinator also requested evaluation information for ongoing improvements to such conferences from the participants, presenters, and other stakeholders. Such interactions among session leaders, faculty members, and other stakeholders can enhance transactions and relevance for participants.

Leaders who guide professional learning sessions typically understand that there are many program decisions and connections of their session participants with related stakeholders, such as funders, cosponsors, and administrators. This chapter provides an overview of many types of learning activities, and Chapter 10 provides additional details on preparation and timing of activities before, during, and following a session. The remainder of this chapter focuses on plans, activities, and connections. Activity leaders and coordinators can select the concepts and examples that best fit their specific session content, goals, and participants from the examples in this overview.

Plans. Effective activity leaders develop guidelines for program decisions to enable them to assist session stakeholders to help plan, conduct, and evaluate a professional learning activity. Explicit guidelines contribute to cooperation and timely decisions. Decisions evolve as leaders and participants become aware of interest in potentially useful session components and then gain access to, find out about, and judge the components' effectiveness, benefits, and potential for future use.

The basic guideline for decisions about activity transactions is that they contribute to active information seeking, decision making, planning, and problem solving by participants regarding their professional performance and quality improvement. Other guidelines for program planning and implementation pertain to the process in which leaders and participants interact, focus on shared program objectives that enhance participants' professional performance, and use ongoing feedback to guide the process and assess outcomes.

Activities. When effective activity leaders select and organize learning sessions, they tend to use some largely implicit guidelines, the first of which is emphasizing active participant engagement in learning activities that enhance professional performance and quality improvement. The second guideline is achieving mutually beneficial exchanges among participants, peers, leaders, helpers, and resource people. The third guideline is gaining agreement on the program agenda and objectives, process, and procedures likely to improve performance. The fourth guideline is providing supportive opportunities to practice and gain mastery of session objectives. The fifth guideline is providing ongoing evaluation feedback to activity stakeholders for purposes of program planning, improvement, and accountability. The sixth guideline is understanding the context in which participants are likely to apply what they gain from the session.

The following is a list of various types of learning activities. Leaders can select combinations best suited for a specific activity or participant group.

1. Self-directed learning project, which may include an arrangement with a mentor regarding scheduling and assistance

2. Individualized mentoring by a coach or guide, which may be informal and voluntary, similar to on-the-job training, and works best when mutually beneficial

3. Peer interaction and networking, such as quality circles, informal discussion, and self-help groups

4. Reading from print and electronic materials, in which participants select topics and decide when to do so

5. Technology-assisted learning, such as cell phones for inquiry and reinforcement, in which electronic connections allow various types of interaction with experts and other participants

6. Weekly spaced activities of about two hours that allow time between sessions for preparation and application

7. Residential conferences, which participants attend full-time for a few days to a week in plenary and concurrent sessions, thus minimizing distractions and maximizing progression

8. Case examples and simulations followed by reflection that emphasize the analysis of complex narratives and participant discovery of underlying concepts and values

Connections. Each of the foregoing activities, singly or in combination, can enable participants to discover personal and situational influences related to professional learning events and their actual performance. Each type of activity can also reveal connections between professional development and performance, including interactions with people in related occupational roles and with people served by the profession. The scope of such connections with people served may focus on one or more scales such as individual, group, organization, community, national, and international. Each scale of connection has many similarities regarding learning transactions as well as some distinctive features. At each level, participants tend to experience a combination of benefits and disadvantages, limitations, and deterrents regarding application of knowledge gained to occupational performance.

Effective activity leaders also realize that sessions and such various scales may have distinctive benefits for provider organizations associated with a professional learning program. For example, a national association conference may enhance solidarity regarding professional values, paired with an enterprise staff development series of weekly sessions, which may enhance interprofessional cooperation, productivity, and computer-enhanced individual preparation for a career transition. In general, effective leaders enhance transactions for session participants by using technology and ongoing evaluation feedback to increase access, provide flexible options, use quality indicators, and improve professional learning sessions that strengthen professional performance.

These comments and examples explain ways effective activity leaders help participants learn by guiding creative interactions, active exchanges to achieve shared objectives, and ongoing feedback to enhance professional performance.

Your reflections on the following questions regarding transactions among leaders and participants can lead to guidelines for initiatives in your specific professional learning session:

1. In the sessions you lead, how interactive are participants with you and each other? If there are any aspects of session activities that should be enhanced, what are they, and what are pertinent concepts regarding such transactions?

2. How else might you improve stakeholder agreement on activity objectives related to professional performance?

3. What more might you do to strengthen transactions (such as opportunities for practice, understanding context, and evaluation feedback) to enhance the learning activity and ongoing professional development?

4. Which options regarding types of active session learning activities might be enhanced, such as self-direction, mentoring, interaction, reading, educational technology, spaced sessions, retreats, and case examples?

5. How might you help participants better understand the combination of benefits and disadvantages associated with various types of learning activities?

6. How might transactions help participants recognize connections between session concepts and their career transactions that can include productivity and interpersonal relations?

9

USING ACTIVE METHODS
WITH PARTICIPANTS

M any activity leaders recognize the importance of using active learning methods. This chapter provides examples and concepts to guide activities that fit program objectives and participants.

Commitment to planning and use of active learning methods are important for activity leaders to emphasize when interacting with participants and coordinators. Effective activity leaders vary in their guiding style, but they usually support and challenge the participants while they use individualized procedures to respond to the diversity of experience and the aspirations of the participants. Active learning includes attention to situational influences, performance, standards, use of technology, encouragement of reflection, and provision of evaluation feedback to guide participants' decisions and application of these elements to enhance professional performance.

After a brief statement of the leadership task, there is an example from the helping professions, followed by various pertinent concepts and some additional examples. The chapter concludes with suggested questions regarding selection of guidelines.

Task: Select, prepare, and use active learning methods and materials that fit program objectives and participants.

Example: An association of community college continuing education administrators conducted professional learning activities for part-time instructors in community college districts. This professional development activity extended over a period of several months, consisting of three live Saturday sessions with a month in between and the use of educational technology before and after each of the Saturday sessions. An experienced association member served as leader of this series, with assistance by one helper for every

25 instructors who enrolled. This enabled the leader and helpers to interact with all participants in subgroups of 10 or fewer through educational technology, as everyone shared their individual plans and expectations.

The leader posted the topics for the group sessions. Participants submitted plans for their own teaching improvement projects and received feedback and suggestions from leaders and other participants. Computer-based education allowed each participant to access readings and examples, engage in simulations and demonstrations, use inquiry procedures to discover how things work, give and receive evaluative feedback on their projects, and submit detailed plans and reports related to aspects of their teaching.

Subgroups of participants were able to focus on content and instructional methods during concurrent subgroup sessions on the three Saturdays during either synchronous prearranged times or asynchronous threaded discussions. This allowed each participant to focus on specific aspects of teaching and learning and to benefit from interactions with interested leaders and participants. Such interactions and networking provided a means for collegial collaboration during and following the four-month professional development program.

In your experience, how unusual is it for participants to have this extent of active learning?

Professional learning activity leaders should reflect on how their sessions can be enhanced by including various roles and methods. Session leaders should emphasize educational methods that entail participant exchanges with peers, leaders, and various resource people and stakeholders. Recruitment and retention of effective session leaders and helpers should emphasize such mutually beneficial exchanges to enhance participation and learning along with organizational collaboration.

A method of achieving such exchanges is to encourage participants to help select agreed-upon intended outcomes related to performance improvement to connect relevant concepts to quality improvement using procedures such as individual coaching, small- and large-group activities, and organizational and community development. Another method is to use various leader perspectives and activity guiding styles that are responsive to diverse participant experiences and aspirations. Yet another method is ongoing evaluation feedback to stakeholders for purposes of planning, improvement, and accountability.

The next examples provide some additional concepts that can be applied to various professional fields.

The leader of a workshop session stated the session's general purpose, followed by brief autobiographical comments by the leader on professional practice and life experience and the importance of values and excellence. This was followed by proposed objectives related to teamwork, guidelines, technology, and decisions. The session included the effective use of visuals, humorous comments, and specific tips for excellent professional performance. Appreciating past mentors, acknowledging practice standards, and responding to the preferences of recipients of participants' professional services were also discussed.

The leader urged participants to avoid a cookie-cutter approach and instead explore options for professional decision making. Then the leader began asking participants for their questions and related comments. The session became increasingly interactive. The leader asked for other viewpoints, suggested asking peers for advice, urged recognition of variations in standards, and observed that some procedures years ago would be done differently today. One participant asked for an unsuccessful example, which the leader provided, and then said that it is important to not only share successes but also have humility and learn from mistakes.

This example involves one activity leader. In the next example from the health field, two very experienced coleaders of an activity had conducted many similar professional learning sessions together over the years. Their planning and joint performance reflected past feedback from various stakeholders and session participants. Thus, their interactions together seemed interchangeable, similar to a performing arts team.

The energy, spontaneity, and humor of this dynamic team led people to refer to them as "the duo." They each visited informally with participants who arrived early not knowing what to expect, which established a rapport with participants. At the start of this informal but fast-paced activity, the duo addressed several themes: Technology and change are affecting the participants' profession and life in general; in spite of some resistance, technology can enable members to effectively and efficiently adhere to professional values. The overview merged smoothly into an initial case example in a series of computer-aided steps, such as diagnosis and modeling. The duo commented on the options available and the advantages and disadvantages of a procedure. In the first hour, the duo presented the case example, referred to concepts from the overview, and provided suggestions about decision-making options and cautions to consider in actual practice.

Participants' discussion of a case example included demonstrations, explanations, and answering questions. At that point, the activity became more hands-on as some helpers used demonstrations, explanations, cautions, humor, and questions and answers to enable participants to practice their use of equipment, tools, materials, and guidelines to conduct and document the aspects of a step-by-step procedure. The duo and helpers circulated among the small groups of participants who were sitting at about 10 tables, asked questions, identified options, mentioned cautions, and adjusted their comments and suggestions according to the participants' stages of familiarity with the tasks.

The duo asked if everyone was progressing well and encouraged them to ask for help. They made the distinction between the previous simulation activity and the actual procedure. They used an overhead projector to show a large image of a small, important detail. Toward the end of the session, the duo provided a brief summary of the main concepts and steps, demonstrated a technique using the projector before participants used the procedure at their table, referred to examples and documentation, and explained that the procedure was iterative so adjustments could easily be made. They concluded with a quip that participants should take away good ideas but return the borrowed equipment. About two dozen participants were still practicing at their tables on additional pieces of equipment at the end, but the duo and helpers continued to assist and to answer questions.

The foregoing examples regarding active learning methods in professional learning sessions illustrate six broad themes for activity leaders to consider: exchange, cooperation, preparation and planning, objectives, activities, and ongoing evaluation feedback. Decisions about methods used by leaders and participants during professional learning activities should focus on transactions in learning sessions between leaders and participants. However, concepts regarding the other five themes illustrate connections with planning, conducting, and evaluating methods.

The first theme is *exchange*. The style and methods of activity leaders are major influences on the exchange between participants and the session leader. It is desirable for exchanges to be mutually beneficial, with each person contributing and learning. In some activities, helpers assist leaders and participants. The energy generated from such interactions can contribute to motivation and engagement during and following a session.

Activity leaders vary in leadership style in general and in the specific methods they select to facilitate active learning. Effective leaders of professional learning sessions recognize that active learning and engagement are especially important and, when successful, reflect multiple influences and consequences. Influences on engagement include participants' motivations regarding what they expect to gain from the professional learning process and its benefits.

Consequences of engaged participation include increased mastery and networking among peers, which contributes to ongoing learning beyond professional learning sessions. The sequence of educational needs assessment, active participation, evaluation feedback, and applying feedback to improve professional performance and quality constitutes an iterative process of successive approximations that reflects changing circumstances that affect performance and change in performance as a result of professional learning activities. An occasional example of current technology illustrates societal trends that influence performance and professional development, as well as the potential enhancement of the process and the results.

Concepts regarding the other five themes can help session leaders facilitate mutually beneficial exchanges as leaders plan, conduct, and evaluate professional learning activities. *Cooperation*, the second theme, is closely associated with exchange because it includes working with multiple stakeholders (such as participants, coordinators, administrators, and funders) and maintaining sustainable accessible cooperation that depends on mutually beneficial communication and interaction.

When stakeholders such as participants, coordinators, or funders contribute to planning professional learning activities, they are more likely to become invested in the effort and its benefits and to help with basic support. This extends to ongoing evaluation feedback, which can encourage stakeholders' use of conclusions. In short, leadership of effective professional learning activities is a team effort instead of a solo performance.

The third theme is *preparation and planning* so that one or a series of professional learning sessions will be responsive to diverse participants who typically vary in their expectations, experience, and preferred learning styles. Diverse participants reflect on available information about the plan for professional learning activities, the extent of the potential match between session characteristics and participants' expectations, and perhaps their unrealistic expectations about the activity process and its benefits. Estimating the assumptions about participants' expectations can include an educational needs assessment before the start of the session and informal contact with some participants so leaders can assess their aspirations and relevant experience.

The fourth theme is *objectives*. Leaders can use relatively accurate estimates of participants' experience, expectations, and preferred learning styles to emphasize or modify their preliminary plan of content related to concepts, examples, and methods.

The purpose of planning is to allow the flexibility to respond to and to achieve more accurate estimates of participants' characteristics. A usual response is to individualize learning activities according to subgroups, pacing, types of activity, and forms of intended use of increased mastery. A by-product of participant engagement is empowerment and individualization, which can also enhance increased proficiency in their professional activities and performance.

Session leader objectives for a professional learning activity should be explored in relation to participant goals and aspirations to clarify shared expectations. Agreement by leaders and participants on the process and outcomes can be a major influence on a session's success. Professional standards can lead to specific guidelines for decisions and emphasis during an activity, along with evaluation. Metaevaluation can include assessment of the desirability and feasibility of session objectives as well as progress toward achieving session objectives.

The fifth theme is *activities*. When professional learning leaders consider learning methods, they understandably focus on the first theme regarding the teaching and learning transactions. Paradoxically, there are many ways to help adults learn, but only a few are actually used in a given session. The ones that are selected typically reflect the leader's experience in guiding sessions, the diversity of participants, and the desired alignment that occurs between session content, objectives, and participant efforts to use such concepts to improve their professional performance.

Methods used by effective activity leaders tend to combine responsiveness to support active engagement and challenges to encourage improvement. Some leaders are able to be supportive and challenging in discussions, questions and answers, demonstrations, and relevant examples. Features of methods that are responsive and allow sufficient practice time for diverse participants include session pacing, distribution of learning activities over multiple sessions, using various types of subgroups, attention to self-directed learning, and references to documentation to encourage interested participants to follow up on specialized topics in greater depth. Leaders should model reflectiveness to encourage participants to explore values, assumptions, viewpoints, and implications related to activity objectives, procedures, roles, and relationships.

The sixth theme is *ongoing evaluation feedback* from program planning, improvement, and accountability. Effective leaders use selective evaluation procedures that are feasible and desirable and share reports with various stakeholders in forms they are likely to understand and use.

Activity leaders should interact with participants to provide a sequence of learning activities to encourage and assist participants to engage actively in sessions. These examples and concepts regarding active learning used by activity leaders include their use of a guiding style that entails individualization for diverse participants, performance standards, and evaluation feedback on behalf of enhanced performance.

Your reflections on the following questions about criteria for participant use of active learning methods and materials can contribute to guidelines in your own specific professional setting:

1. How can agreement on activity objectives and professional standards energize participants' engagement?
2. What methods and materials that you use for exchanges with participants contribute most to their active engagement? How do you encourage participants to relate content to their personal performance and circumstances? How might you enhance the process and future learning activities for even more beneficial exchanges?
3. How might your activities contribute to supporting and challenging participants through discussions, questions, and examples? What more might you do by way of modeling, pacing, forming subgroups, creating simulations, encouraging reflections, using technology, and promoting self-directed learning to enhance active learning during and after sessions?
4. How might past and future activity planning contribute to responsiveness to diverse participant backgrounds and expectations, including leader flexibility, presentation of options, contributions by mentors, and encouragement of reflection?
5. How might cooperation with and among participants and other stakeholders enrich active engagement, practice, and learning? In what ways does evaluation feedback contribute to active participant learning to reinforce progress, quality improvement, and ongoing professional development?

10

SEQUENCING ACTIVITIES FOR PROGRESS

Effective professional development leaders plan and conduct activities by selecting and organizing learning sessions with contributions from the participants and other stakeholders. The leadership task on transactions in the previous chapter included options for learning activities. This component on concepts and examples guides decisions about sequencing learning activities early in a session or midway, late, and following a session. Typically, activity leaders are central to such decisions along with contributions from coordinators and participants.

The concepts and examples on sequencing explain ways effective activity leaders begin with a flexible plan, make decisions about activities in the sequence, include options to be responsive to diverse participants, guide ongoing evaluation and reflection, and emphasize improving performance.

After a brief statement of the leadership task, there is an example from the helping professions, followed by various pertinent concepts and some additional examples. The chapter concludes with suggested questions regarding selection of guidelines.

Task: Discuss why and how to sequence session activities.

Example: Some states have intermediate school districts of cooperative educational services that oversee staff development for teachers and administrators in the district. Activities within easy distance, planned and conducted by staff, contribute to keeping costs low and benefits high. Usually, a local staff member who chairs a planning committee obtains suggestions from interested staff members to estimate participation, selects topics and methods, and suggests the remaining steps for planning a session or two. A usual schedule for a session is two Saturdays between midmorning and midafternoon, two weeks apart. Because potential participants are from nearby school districts, transportation is not a problem.

The following proposed sequence of activities might emerge from a planning committee meeting after the content has been agreed upon:

1. A month or more before the first Saturday session, send participants a draft of the program's purpose and topics and a short questionnaire about their expectations.
2. A week before the first Saturday session, send participants a brief summary of initial concepts to consider and several questions to be discussed at the first session.
3. Be sure the opening hour of the first Saturday session includes the welcome address, introductions, and orientation.
4. Build the agenda for the day's topics.
5. Analyze a case example, followed by discussion in subgroups on local applications.
6. Provide evaluation and feedback from the first Saturday, with implications for individual follow-up during the intervening two weeks and suggestions for the second Saturday session.
7. Reflect on the sequence of professional development topics and activities so far and discuss implications for future directions and benefits from ongoing reinforcement.
8. Send summary comments and preliminary plans for the second Saturday session at least a week before.

Note. The second Saturday session should reflect the progress and feedback to date.

The foregoing example includes concepts such as participant preparation before an activity, agreement on program goals early in the process, increased emphasis on evaluation feedback later in the session, and discussion of plans for future professional learning activities.

The following case example illustrates additional concepts to guide sequencing of session activities, such as educational technology, observations and demonstrations early and later in a session, attention to varied practice opportunities, and relevance to improved performance.

This example illustrates live electronic interaction between a university surgery department's operating rooms and participants at a remote location one hour away with a total of about 100 people during a two-day conference on general surgery. The operating rooms were equipped with technology for the session. The session leader welcomed the opportunity to coordinate all aspects of planning, conducting, and evaluating the session.

This coordination included working with a planning committee, clarifying the focus on understanding the surgical procedures selected because the planners believed they were likely to be of interest to participants. The planning also included review of past participants' comments, and review of clinical practice and potential case examples to be demonstrated during the session. The session leader worked with instructional technology staff and potential attending surgeons to help conduct the session.

A member of the surgical team served as case director for electronic connections between people in the operating room and the conference participants at a remote location. The case director and other planning committee members were aware of the general sequence of events during the hourlong live session. The session leader was at the front of the conference room to guide the discussion. Two operating rooms, each with the surgical team and a patient, were connected electronically. This allowed conference participants to witness surgical procedures and discuss the procedures and rationale of the surgical team as they would if they were actually in the operating room. Having patients undergoing surgery in each of the two operating rooms allowed interactions with conference participants before, during, and following the surgical procedure. Evaluation feedback from people in each role indicated that case selection and logistics at the department and the conference venues worked smoothly.

Selecting and organizing learning activities to achieve session objectives is essential to leading professional learning activities and quality improvement. Concepts from other program development leadership tasks can encourage leaders to reflect on their habitual ways of conducting sessions and identify ways to improve the process. The transaction components focus is on planning and selecting potential learning activities.

This component on sequencing provides guidelines for activity leaders and planners to use when deciding on the mix of activities to use early, in the middle, and late in the program and to modify the sequence and emphasis as an activity progresses. While other stakeholders, such as coordinators, administrators, and technology specialists, may contribute to planning decisions, typically the leader and participants decide on the sequence of the program. This allows session activity to be responsive to participants' experience and feedback during the successive stages of a learning activity.

Several guidelines regarding sequencing activities should be considered during early planning to provide flexibility for leaders and participants to make decisions about a session or series of sessions based on participants' evolving proficiency and applying the information to improve performance. The first guideline is providing options that allow for responsiveness based on the leader's increasing recognition, early in the activity, of variations in the capability and application opportunities of the participants. Modifications and options could be applied to topics and methods.

A second guideline is consideration of alternative logistics (such as facilities, technology, and an agenda with uncommitted time), which allows activities to be modified for all or for subgroups of participants.

The third guideline is inclusion of some force-field analysis of likely positive and negative influences, such as costs and benefits related to available resources, so, as an activity progresses, it will be feasible for the leader to make desirable modifications. It can be very frustrating for leaders to be unable to make important but minor improvements in learning activities because of a lack of facilities or resources that could have been easily planned for. The remaining guidelines for sequencing involve preparation, interaction, and conclusion.

Preparation. Effective leaders understand the desirability of exchanging information with participants before the start of the learning activity. This guideline includes providing participants with advance information shortly before a session, such as an overview of additional details about the session's purpose and content. It also includes requesting participants to consider their expectations in more detail and to send the leader their suggestions, which may have been prompted by the overview. One potential result of this exchange is to encourage participants to take initiative and participate in exchanges during and following the activity.

Interaction. The fundamental guideline regarding sequencing during the professional learning activity is for the leader to have a flexible plan for the beginning, middle, and end of the activity, which can be modified based on emerging conclusions about participant characteristics and expectations. Effective leaders combine their experience from similar programs, along with suggested guidelines, to prepare a flexible program plan that reflects information from potential participants and other stakeholders. Usual basic plans include an early orientation such as an agreement on goals and procedures, followed by a series of activities for phased practice for increased mastery or achievement of program objectives, and conclude with reflections on progress and participants' commitment to continued efforts to enhance professional performance. Feedback throughout a session based on aspects of ongoing evaluation and monitoring such as diversity, technology, and individual initiatives enables leaders to interact with participants and other pertinent stakeholders to modify activities.

The following are guidelines for flexible sequencing of session activities:

1. Include an orientation, welcoming comments, and an introduction so participants feel comfortable interacting in a supportive and challenging activity.
2. Build on positive first impressions of the learning activity to explore and agree on relevant activity objectives and arrangements to accommodate major differences in backgrounds and expectations to progress toward the achievement of program objectives.
3. Provide an overview and brief rationale for the sequence of activities for all participants, subgroups, and any individual self-directed efforts.
4. Use brief presentations, observations, and demonstrations to enable participants to build on their current proficiency (knowledge, skills, and attitudes) and explore directions for increased mastery. Questions and discussions can reinforce major concepts, identify desirable resources and materials, and increase interactions in whole-group, subgroup, and individual conversations.
5. Decide on the extent of preparation assistance or type of participant engagement to provide participants based on their apparent experience with technology and materials. Then proceed to more complex and interactive benefits such as case analysis and simulation, and finally emphasize the application of these benefits to improved professional performance. Along with inquiry and discovery as participants analyze examples, prompt decisions, and evaluate progress and results, leaders should guide individual or group reflection regarding assumptions, values, alternatives, outcomes, and especially similarities and differences between the examples and the actual features of related professional performance. Opportunities to practice and reflect on new concepts and procedures should be relevant and varied to achieve increased mastery.
6. Review evaluation feedback and informal impressions regarding participants' progress toward achievement of program objectives; the major learning procedures; contributions of technology, materials, and facilities; and individualization of professional learning efforts during and following the activity.

Conclusion. After a session or series of sessions, a leader can encourage participants to continue their professional learning efforts, for example, by sending a general activity summary as a reminder, providing encouraging suggestions for continued progress, reminding participants of the individual action plans they prepared during the activity, requesting their progress reports on their application of program insights to improve performance, sending them prompts to encourage application of these insights, and informing them of upcoming professional learning activities that might interest them.

Experienced professional learning activity leaders tend to develop guidelines for planning a flexible responsive sequence of activities to guide the content, objectives, and participants' preparation. Early planning typically includes estimates of participants' abilities and aspirations, which sometimes include participants' preparation, before beginning the group session and individualized learning activities, based on estimates of educational needs of participants and others.

Agreement on activity objectives and basic procedures can facilitate cooperation and suggest resources for active engagement in learning activities. Effective activities can provide learning opportunities for a realistic session and questions to guide participants' preparation for excellent performance. It is also important for participants to gain an understanding of ways to recognize and reduce resistance to change. Ongoing evaluation feedback can include continued learning related to professional development beyond session activities.

The following questions about sequencing learning activities are intended to encourage your reflection on guidelines for your specific session:

1. What more might you do during planning committee meetings and especially program planning to preserve flexibility to respond to unexpected influences and opportunities during an activity?
2. What information do you usually exchange with participants so they can contribute to interaction during and following an activity?
3. How else might participants gain an overview of program goals and activities that clarify sequencing of activities for all participants, subgroups, and individual efforts?
4. What are some innovative ways to vary practice opportunities that encourage persistence by participants during and following an activity?
5. What more can you discover about diverse participant characteristics and aspirations that could enhance activity goals and procedures?
6. How might ongoing evaluation feedback during an activity help stakeholders assist participants to better connect to improved performance and their session activities, such as case analysis and simulations?
7. How can you encourage ongoing reflection by participants?

8. In what ways do presentations, observations, and demonstrations help participants build on their current proficiencies and explore future directions?

9. How else might participants be encouraged to continue professional learning activities, such as summaries of types of improvements in performance, contextual analysis of situational influences on performance, potential uses of educational technology available to continue learning after a session, action plans, and progress reports?

PART FOUR

EVALUATING SESSION PLANS, IMPROVEMENTS, RESULTS, RESOURCES, AND INFLUENCES

R egarding the connections in chapters 11 and 12 on evaluating session plans, improvements, results, resources, and influences: The tasks in these chapters occur before, during, and following sessions on resources and influences along with ongoing evaluation feedback to stakeholders.

11

PROVIDING EVALUATION FEEDBACK TO STAKEHOLDERS

Effective session leaders and coordinators recognize that people associated in any way with a professional learning activity tend to make informal judgments about the experience but seldom share their conclusions and the criteria on which they are based. The examples and concepts in this chapter suggest ways activity leaders can make more explicit the program evaluation process, conclusion, and feedback to stakeholders.

Effective leaders plan, conduct, and use evaluation conclusions to guide decisions related to program goals, participants, activities, and improved professional performance. Major evaluation concepts include building on relevant publications about evaluation to select aspects of the program on which to focus; helping participants judge ways to use learning to enhance performance, including multiple stakeholders in the evaluation planning for program improvement and accountability; deciding on session objectives and activities; and emphasizing ongoing evaluation feedback useful to leaders and participants for conducting interactive sessions.

After a brief statement of the leadership task, there is an example from the helping professions, followed by various pertinent concepts and some additional examples. The chapter concludes with suggested questions regarding selection of guidelines.

Task: Explore ways to effectively provide ongoing evaluation feedback to professional learning activity stakeholders (participants, leaders, coordinators, administrators, funders, collaborators, policymakers).
Example: A professional development proposal for strengthening collaboration among public health professionals included ongoing evaluation.

A feature of the proposal was interprofessional education for nurses (public health agencies, schools), physicians (primary care, public health, prevention), and people in related occupations (concerned with wellness, prevention, environment, security, and collaboration).

Evaluation for the multiyear funded project allowed ongoing feedback from multiple stakeholders regarding professional learning procedures and outcomes to guide program decisions and to demonstrate innovative ways for stakeholders to obtain and use evaluation conclusions. Experience with similar evaluation efforts had shown that stakeholders' actual use of evaluation conclusions was the other half of the challenge. A report from a brief survey on similar public health professional development projects helped identify promising goals, procedures, examples, and resources. This led to the assembly of baseline information about current occupations, stakeholders, cooperation, professional development, and applying conclusions in the region.

Some of the conclusions contributed to an evaluability assessment to guide the selection of evaluation topics and methods. Time series data regarding commitments, interventions, and use of evaluation feedback helped monitor trends and guide decisions by people associated with the funded project. Local case study narratives helped explain how things worked and suggested promising interventions. A special focus was the linkage between the resource systems (public health professionals) and client systems (patients and especially families and neighborhoods served) regarding prevention and wellness. Information about the timing, detail, focus, and stakeholder use of evaluation feedback was a special benefit of the project, which external funding and metaevaluation helped make feasible.

The following example of professional development and a hospital-based clinical specialty illustrates additional uses of evaluation:

A goal of this clinical example is learning to think and reflect before, during, and following a procedure so that participants learn to become more able to engage in observation, self-assessment, and critical thinking. This type of clinical teaching also calls for unusual forms of evaluation feedback that are connected with performance. During the several years when participants go through their clinical preparation, it is important to them and to the leader and other faculty members to have valid and reliable evaluation feedback. The combination of various able practitioners, years of preparation, and evaluation procedures on which participants' scores are clustered at the top makes it difficult to rank participants.

Several assessment procedures have been used, including an evaluation form with objective, behavioral, and cognitive standards with more than two dozen items rated on a 9-point scale. Another procedure uses a standardized case with multiple faculty members who score student performance. This procedure can be difficult to achieve with high interrater reliability. Providing leaders' feedback to participants can guide their progress and prepare them for formal examinations, which are an important part of their career advancement.

The foregoing examples provide some guidelines to help session leaders and coordinators understand why and how to help stakeholders assist with planning, conducting, and using cost-effective program evaluations. The following overview suggests ways to conduct program evaluation and feedback related to all components of professional development planning, progress, and results, which are context, outlook, stakeholders, objectives, outcomes, activities, and process.

Context. For some professional learning session evaluation efforts, it is desirable to include relevant information about contextual influences on the learning and evaluation process. It is especially important to include influences related to the local service area where participants are likely to use what they learn. Conclusions on contextual influence are likely to include potential participants' opinions and influences on the willingness of potential stakeholders to cooperate. Because participants are the primary stakeholders, conclusions from contextual analysis are especially valuable for understanding opportunities, expectations, and deterrents to progress. Information about external influences may be especially important when sessions include interprofessional education and international comparative perspectives. Contextual analysis conclusions can also guide decisions about desirable program offerings, outcomes, educational activities, and an efficient and beneficial evaluation process.

Outlook. An educational needs assessment is the usual type of evaluation for planning. The assessment can provide estimates of participant readiness along with additional levels of mastery, motives, and expectations. Ongoing evaluation findings can monitor participant commitment, increasing mastery and application to actual performance, satisfaction, and reflection on earlier assumptions regarding progress and future directions. Increased understanding of diverse participant educational needs and circumstances can enhance the identification of relevant stakeholders, appropriate objectives, responsive educational activities, and the ongoing evaluation process and procedures for feedback to guide stakeholder decisions.

Stakeholders. Evaluation conclusions are of limited value unless they are used. Early in program development, evaluation findings can help identify examples of participants, peers, instructors, coordinators, and other potential stakeholders whose involvement in planning a program might strengthen the plan and its implementation. Increased understanding of an evaluation of stakeholder values, resources, and anticipated benefits of the exchange—along with satisfactory procedures, interpersonal relations, and agreements among multiple stakeholders—can enhance stakeholder decisions. This engagement is especially valuable because the main challenge in evaluation pertains to stakeholders' use of conclusions.

Objectives. Evaluation conclusions regarding contacts, outlooks, stakeholder capabilities, and interests can help leaders select high-priority general program goals to provide a sense of direction for joint planning. If similar programs had been provided earlier, the objective-setting process might include evaluating past accomplishments to determine what was actually accomplished and what was not.

Sometimes relevant professional practice standards and evidence related to guidelines can be reflected in intended outcomes. Especially when there are diverse potential participants who work in various settings, the program planners may have little influence on actual professional performance in the workplace, so the outcome focus may be on participants' proficiency (combination of knowledge, skills, and attitudes), which constitutes the capability and commitment to achieve high-quality expert performance, given the opportunity.

Clear and realistic educational objectives are fundamental to guide program decisions about achievable occupational performance indicators, educational activities to aid progress, and educational process indicators to assess improvements, performance outcomes, and plans for using evaluation feedback to stakeholders.

Outcomes. All stakeholders care about evaluation findings on the impact and the results of professional learning activities. Stakeholders such as administrators and funders are especially interested in evidence about the types and extent of such outcomes and benefits, such as career advancement, enhanced professional performance, and improved benefits for people served by professionals. Programs provided by associations and educational institutions typically focus on individual professionals, whereas human resource development activities provided by enterprises where professionals interact in the worksite typically focus on organizational development and quality improvement.

Most professional learning and quality improvement objectives and activities occur over time, although individual sessions may be short term and focus on a stage of longer-term improvements. Evaluation of outcomes can include time-series collection and analysis of data to assess levels of performance and effectiveness, judge the extent of sustained improvement, analyze the influences that helped or hindered improvement, and provide feedback on implications to inform stakeholder decisions. Ongoing evaluation of the impact on actual outcomes and organizational benefits can occur not only for needs assessment and planning but also during the educational activities, for purposes of improvement, and at the conclusion of the learning sessions. Communicating conclusions and implications should be targeted to fit the recipients.

Activities. In practice, most professional learning session evaluations are limited to participant and instructor satisfaction with the educational activities. Such conclusions are useful but largely ignore the six aspects of evaluation and the many decisions about the educational activity that are central to its effectiveness. Part of the reason for this limited focus on satisfaction with learning activities is the seemingly daunting complexity of a more comprehensive evaluation. An evaluability assessment generally selects only some aspects of a professional learning activity as the focus of the full evaluation. For efficient and useful program evaluation, leadership is important to help stakeholders better understand important relationships and results to guide their decisions. The following are aspects of an activity that should be evaluated:

1. Relevance of content
2. Use of educational technology
3. Diversity of participants
4. Orientation of session instructors
5. Interactive sessions that emphasize active learning
6. Efficient evaluations to guide program decisions, including feedback, reinforcement, and empowering participants for ongoing professional development

Process. Publications on educational evaluation include suggestions for the technical process of planning, conducting, and reporting as well as information about the program. Evaluation planning includes deciding which of the many objectives a specific program evaluation can address, such as scale, focus, samples, qualitative and quantitative data, cross-validation from multiple sources, peer review, before-and-after comparisons, longitudinal trends, attention to processes and outcomes, feedback reported to stakeholders, benefits, assessment of the evaluation technology, and depth of analysis of the educational quality improvement procedures.

It is especially important to include people with evaluation expertise who can contribute to decisions related to the foregoing options and procedures. Evaluation leadership can enhance professional development in several ways, such as drawing sound conclusions for decisions; using a manageable scale; fitting program decisions and available resources; engaging stakeholders in the evaluation process to encourage the use of evaluation conclusions and implications for future sessions; and using evaluation to assess the quality of the plans, procedures, findings, evaluators, and benefits from evaluation that justify the cost.

Session leaders can use the concepts and examples in this chapter to provide ongoing evaluation feedback for stakeholder decisions regarding session objectives, activities, and practices to help improve professional performance. Publications, advice, and your experience with evaluation concepts and procedures can enable leaders to select the program aspects that are likely to enhance activity process and results.

Your reflections on the following questions can contribute to the creation of guidelines for your specific session:

1. What might an evaluation aimed at previous similar learning activities for participants from diverse occupational settings contribute to your decisions and to the feedback to stakeholders about performance indicators, useful activities, content, and procedures?

2. How do you (and the evaluation specialist who may assist you) make decisions about evaluation scale, resources, future directions, and stakeholders' use of conclusions?

3. How else might you use feasible contextual analysis to increase understanding of opportunities, expectations, and deterrents to guide session decisions about program objectives, activities, and evaluation processes?

4. To what extent do your conclusions from program evaluation help guide your decisions about content relevance, educational technology, participant diversity, instructor orientation, active learning, and efficient evaluations?

5. How are you using conclusions from the assessment of activity participants' educational needs to guide decisions regarding participant commitment, increasing mastery, application to performance, and future directions?

6. How might you include stakeholders in the evaluation planning and use of conclusions?

7. What have your recent assessment conclusions about outcomes contributed to your understanding of participants' career advancement and enhanced performance and benefits to the people served by professionals that could guide your decisions about participants' sustained performance improvement, major influences, and feedback to participants?

8. What did you learn from evaluation findings about stakeholders' values, contributions, and benefits that could guide decisions about activity procedures, interpersonal relations, and cooperation?

12

RECOGNIZING CONTEXTUAL INFLUENCES

In addition to multiple influences on professional performance, there are contextual influences on learning activities. Recognizing such influences is a distinctive contribution of session leaders who can explain the importance of contextual influences, the types of influences, and their implications on professional learning activities.

Activity leaders and other stakeholders can clarify and share information about various situational influences on learning sessions, in addition to contextual influences on professional performance and personal influences on their sessions. Activity leaders, coordinators, and participants can help explain multiple external influences on participation, such as program image, deterrents, attraction, retention, participation, application of knowledge gained, providers, and collaboration.

Activity leaders and coordinators can be especially helpful regarding the interpretation of indicators of contextual influences, organizational culture, resources, program learning climate, technology, media, and relation to professional performance. Activity stakeholders can plan, conduct, and share the results of inquiry projects and proposals as external assistance to innovative efforts that enhance professional learning sessions.

After a brief statement of the leadership task, there is an example from the helping professions, followed by various pertinent concepts and some additional examples. The chapter concludes with suggested questions regarding selection of guidelines.

Task: Recognize contextual influences on professional development activities.
Example: Contextual influences are especially central for some types of activities.

Part of the extension mission of some universities is assistance in solving local community problems. The geographic area for a series of sessions may be a city, several rural counties, the whole state, a multistate region, or another country. Typically, a community development specialist helps local people help themselves with public issues.

Often, an emerging issue that elicits contrasting views from local stakeholders prompts a request for assistance by a specialist who can help them analyze the symptoms and causes of the issue, identify resources and options, and work together to chart desirable directions based on shared values. The specific issue may pertain to economic development, public health, natural resources, regional planning, population shifts, or educational opportunities.

The leader of the local university community development office devoted a daylong activity for specialists from throughout the state to discuss their views on how to help local residents deal with situational influences at successive stages of the community development process. Some of the influences included how various segments of the community view the symptoms of the issue, acceptance of the concept of including multiple stakeholders in the community development process, economic and population trends, extent of trust and shared values, local history of conflict and distrust among subpopulations, and availability of local leadership during and following the discussion of the issue.

The activity leader included simulations and other participatory activities for interaction and sharing that would enable new and experienced specialists to analyze and reflect on the concepts, skills, and feelings each participant could adapt to the issue as they assisted local residents with community development issues in their area.

People with experience guiding such learning activities recognize that multiple influences affect session leaders and participants. The following example focuses on members of an organization:

Quality improvement (QI) efforts in an enterprise are especially likely to analyze external influences on staff development. One member of the human resource development staff of a wholesale enterprise had a special interest in leadership responsibility for QI activities. The QI leader's efforts were guided by current performance, quality standards, evaluation feedback, staff initiatives, and recognition of benefits from QI achievements. Sources of information about performance included work records, observation and representative interviews with staff and their supervisors, guidelines about standards, related quality indicators from various locations, QI reports from the wholesale enterprise, and suggestions from quality circle teams in various departments of the enterprise.

Ongoing 360-degree assessments of process and outcomes of work performance and QI efforts were compiled monthly from the multiple sources of assessment and distributed in separate forms to various stakeholders. Staff initiatives regarding ways to improve quality were encouraged by slogans such as "Quality Is Everyone's Responsibility"; periodic reports from QI teams; and responses to QI suggestions by staff members; and quarterly and annual QI reports and announcements that highlighted benefits to individuals, work teams, and the entire enterprise.

Trustworthy communication provided a foundation for specific QI activities in this learning organization. The key QI leader privately noted indicators of trust and communication, management priorities, and supervisor actions likely to influence the QI mission. These private notes helped inform the leader's annual plan of work as well as potential influences on occupational and work team performance.

Which features of this example were most likely to contribute to the quality improvement leader's understanding of external influences on staff development?

Session leaders can help participants understand the importance of influences and activities in a series of learning sessions. Multiple influences on community and organization development are typical, so how many and what types of indicators are important for leaders to address? The potential benefits from understanding situational influences can vary with the stakeholders. Session participants may analyze influences in a case example, a session leader may guide the discussion, and a session coordinator may analyze influences on past sessions to apply results to future sessions.

People tend to take contextual influences for granted, as reflected in the adage that fish lack a concept of water because they are always surrounded by it. Then, why do some professional learning session leaders give explicit attention to situational trends and issues that they assume to be important to participants' understanding and performance? The following overview of concepts regarding contextual influences illustrates some of the indicators leaders might consider.

The essence of leadership generally is to encourage stakeholders to embrace shared goals and contribute to achievement of those goals. Most professional learning activity leaders assume that participants' learning is central to enhanced performance and quality improvement. Many participants take for granted that their professional roles include contextual influences on their performance as well as their efforts to influence the people in the groups they serve.

Indicators of progress by participants and benefits to people, groups, organizations, and communities include some explicit attention to external influences. But how many and what types of contextual indicators are important for leaders to address? The short answer to this question is enough to understand major connections to decisions on professional learning activities.

For example, some learning programs focus narrowly on mastery of technical procedures that could be used in various settings with little attention to broader economic, social, and policy issues. By contrast, in other sessions, understanding and addressing contextual influences and trends such as organizational support, proposed legislation, and media images closely connected to performance may be central to program objectives. Force-field analysis can contribute eye-opening insights. As illustrated by the Serenity Prayer, effective leaders should recognize which issues are relevant, which are not, and have the wisdom to know the difference.

It may take but a few questions by leaders and other stakeholders engaged in session planning to recognize the scope, depth, and importance of the contextual issues that should be considered. The potential benefits of increased understanding of contextual influences related to professional learning activities vary with the stakeholders. A program leader may analyze influences on session planning and implementation and on participants' professional learning during and following the activity. A coordinator may analyze influences on past sessions that have implications for future activities. Participants may benefit from a greater understanding of situational demands and constraints related to their performance, career, and quality improvement.

Participants may also want to know more about trends and issues that influence the people they serve, so they can serve them better. This may be especially important for helping professionals who want to help people help themselves. As leaders gain new insights about such influences, they can reflect on implications for decisions by themselves and other stakeholders, and on contrasting views that various people may have about the importance of the resulting implications. The impact of contextual influences on activities and stakeholders can be great because of complex connections. Examples include media; organizations; technology; and social, demographic, cultural, economic, and political influences.

Leaders' use of concepts about contextual influences is typically related to program content and procedures. Leaders' understanding of important influences relevant to learning activities can enable them to explain to other stakeholders why such explicit understanding is desirable in relation to the professional field and decisions they might make. Recognition of major contextual influences on learning opportunities can enhance their perception of relative costs and benefits and can affect their choices. Members' values and circumstances can encourage some people to attend a session because it might provide continued learning. However, results from educational needs assessment with potential participants can be another useful source of insights about influences. How might a session leader and participants cooperate to select, analyze, and use conclusions about situational influences on their professional learning activity? What discourages participation by other members? An example is using educational technology to increase access. Following basic marketing guidelines can help leaders and stakeholders recognize and share values and increase cooperation.

Participatory activities such as discussing examples, case analyses, simulations, learning communities, and organizational analysis of strengths, weaknesses, opportunities and threats are especially valuable ways to increase systemic understanding of contextual influences.

In contrast to many professional development activities that focus on procedures such as innovation or acquisition of resources, or outcomes and results, analysis of contextual influences on professional learning helps make explicit the interplay of positive and negative influences as well as efforts by professionals to guide changes in their group, organizational, or societal context. Such insights can also alert professionals to current and potential forms of feedback that can indicate the extent and types of influence that help and hinder professional learning efforts.

A central question for session leaders is, What are major influences on members regarding their participation in professional learning activities? Clearly, there are various personal and situational influences on participation.

Most participants appreciate session arrangements that can be conveniently accessed and include discussions of how to apply what they have learned. However, they are unlikely to explore influences on their learning activities unless some assistance is provided.

The following are examples of ways a leader can better understand participants' perceptions of influences on their professional learning activities:

1. Respond to inquiries about the change events and educational needs that prompted their initial and ongoing participation.
2. Comment about influences on the process of their participation.
3. Refer to ways their past experiences affected their professional learning efforts.

4. List indicators of the combination of personal and situational influences on their persistence in professional learning activities.
5. Explain what helps and what hinders their efforts to apply and use what they gain from professional learning activities.
6. Obtain information about their perception of the relative influence on their decisions to participate from program information (brochures, e-mails, announcements) and from informal sources (encouragement from past experience, organizational cosponsorship).
7. Use session-related publications before, during, and following a session.

There are additional ways leaders can better understand influences on their learning activities. Much depends on a leader's experience with topics such as professional performance, educational technology, obtaining resources for their session, and assessing specific influences on their learning activity. Leaders who are interested can learn about influences by themselves or can involve other session stakeholders, such as participants and coordinators.

The extent and type of sessions that asssess influences on professional learning tend to reflect perceptions of the relevance and utility of the conclusions for decisions about program planning, improvement, accountability, and evaluation feedback to stakeholders.

The following example illustrates a county public health nurse's efforts to increase public and financial support for professional development:

This effort of a public health nurse focused on ways to increase the effectiveness of various health professionals. The nurse's professional development efforts were greatly influenced by two trends: the growing number of problems that residents and enterprises in the county experienced related to public health issues and the steady decline in funding and supportive policies for public health. About a decade earlier, the nurse had recognized that progress would entail some form of collaboration and consolidation.

Preliminary contact was made with people from various occupations who had participated in professional learning activities and seemed receptive to explore increased interprofessional cooperation. The success of Heartbeat Wales regarding collaborative efforts to reduce risk factors related to cardiovascular illness indicated to the nurse that greater collaboration was desirable and feasible.

A loosely coupled interprofessional network of public health professionals in the county included people associated with health departments, health professional associations, university health professions schools, media, volunteers interested in health issues, and state legislators and administrators who were supportive of improved public health services.

Gradually, this cooperative effort led to broad support for improved policies and financial support for public health improvement. This progress encouraged the leader's counterparts in some other counties to initiate similar efforts, which contributed to improved state support as well.

One type of external influence on an activity is technology. The following example of a workshop session focuses on digital technology for professional practice:

The activity leader described the leader's personal use of the technology during the previous three years, demonstrated the main features, and then guided the participants' discussion during the session. When providing some personal and professional background information, the leader commented that working in a group practice allowed specialization in using digital technology.

The leader said that current digital technology could produce more accurate results in less time and then played a DVD on a professional process using the digital technology. Then the leader asked participants to state their expectations for the session, assured them that the session would cover their main expectations, and proceeded to summarize the session objectives. PowerPoint slides were then used to describe five main aspects of the process and the main benefits.

During the next hour, successive case examples were used to explain the transfer of digital documentation to a website, creation and use of 3-D models, comparison of a digital simulation with an actual 3-D model, digital technology related to stakeholder interaction, and use of standards of excellence to compare with actual conditions to guide decision making.

At this point, participants were asked about their experience with the process they used, followed by comments from the leader to reinforce and enhance their comments. In response to numerous questions from participants, the leader cited sources of more detailed information and shared observations on current and future developments in the field. The leader then raised the room lights during the remainder of the session for a demonstration and opportunity for participants to practice using the digital technology.

The demonstration reviewed highlights from earlier in the session and foreshadowed the procedures that participants would soon use for realistic practice. Small groups of participants alternated practicing the procedure, assessing, and observing while waiting their turn to practice. Throughout this stage of the activity, the leader commented about the balance between speed and accuracy, improving performance through a combination of skill and knowledge and attitude, and the value of feedback. The concluding minutes of the activity included sharing humorous comments, expressing appreciation for contributions from more experienced participants, and identifying connections between topics and workshop objectives and participant expectations.

How did this session leader guide participants' understanding of relationships between technology and the session activities?

Sometimes collaboration provides an effective way to deal with various contextual influences. When two or three provider organizations cooperate on a professional learning activity, usually one type of organization may be the provider and the other organizations assist. Such instances may be very similar to having a solo provider, but it is important to understand the cooperating contributions and expectations of the assisting organizations. However, when there is a more formal collaboration or consortium, the leader should analyze specific organizational dynamics, especially interpersonal relations among people from one or more professions, regarding cooperation and expectations.

Sustained partnerships usually benefit from three major features: shared interests, distinctive contributions, and equitable benefits. Leaders who appreciate the dynamics of such concepts in a specific situation are able to estimate influences on cooperation and how they may influence connections to improve sessions and participants' ongoing professional learning. Sometimes it is important to help participants explore explicit connections between provider organization dynamics and desirable goals of the activity, along with their personal professional learning expectations.

Proposals to obtain additional resources for a series of professional learning activities include useful concepts and procedures in general. The proposal process may be formal when soliciting potential resources from the provider organization or from external sources such as funding agencies and organizational collaborations. In each instance, success is more likely when the leader or coordinator analyzes information about the mission of the potential source of assistance and aligns its proposal with the mission and incentives of the donor. It is usually a good investment of time for an activity leader and coordinator to explore, review, analyze, and reflect on information about potential donors' mission, priorities, and characteristics.

Sometimes a useful starting point is a focused inquiry in which leaders can select one or two research and evaluation methodological concepts and procedures to increase understanding of how the selected aspects of professional learning work. Illustrative methods and procedures include observation, interviews, focus groups, questionnaires, simulations, literature reviews, and comparative analyses of case examples. The resulting reports can be enhanced by including an inquiry team of people from several stakeholder categories who might help use the conclusions to guide planning and conduct more effective professional learning activities.

Potential resources and support to conduct such inquiry projects can be enhanced by using a proposal (including project costs and benefits) and a rationale that aligns the inquiry project with systemic features of the professional learning activities that might be enhanced by applying the intended project conclusions. Sometimes collaboration between the organization that conducts professional learning activities and related organizations can increase cooperation, resources, and session effectiveness.

With all the efforts to seek greater understanding of external influences on professional learning activities, it is important to include disseminating and sharing conclusions with stakeholders to strengthen current programs and enhance planning for future activities.

The foregoing concepts and examples are initiatives activity stakeholders can take to better explain external influences on participants, sessions, the learning climate, innovation, inquiry, and proposals for acquisition of resources to enhance creative professional learning activities.

The following questions should help you decide how to better understand indicators of situational influences on a specific session that warrant further analysis of the influences and implications for conducting a session, and ways to enable participants to use their understanding of situational influences as they plan and conduct future professional learning sessions:

1. How might you connect pertinent concepts about organizational dynamics to decisions about a specific learning activity, such as guiding participant inquiry, encouraging interaction among diverse participants, conducting comparative case analysis, and paying attention to organizational dynamics in session evaluation criteria?

2. How should greater and more explicit recognition of external influences on an activity enable leaders and participants to increase relevance regarding professional learning and occupational performance? Why are contributions by leaders and coordinators especially important in this regard? How might you conduct activities (such as case examples and simulations) that can be especially valuable ways to make contextual influences on activities explicit for participants?

3. What types of external influences on activities are important to address for a specific event? (Options for seeking participants' perspectives on influences include what triggered their decision to participate in the session, the impact on their professional development, and their application of insights from the session.)

4. What are promising ways to obtain useful information about influences on activities? (Examples of procedures include quality improvement standards, evaluation reports from similar sessions, and conclusions regarding administrative priorities and resource allocations.)

5. What questions regarding influences on activities might be included in assessment reports, and what procedures might be used? (Examples of procedures include observations, interviews, questionnaires, and case examples.) What are cost-beneficial ways to analyze external influences that can take into account procedures and benefits, such as connections with media, organizations, technology, and societal trends, as well as how conclusions can be used to enhance mutually beneficial exchanges?

6. Have you recognized similarities and differences between internal and external sources of support? Have your requests for pilot project funding included provisions for supplemental support beyond the initial assistance?

7. Has your search for enhanced human resources included attracting people with expertise in technology, session content, marketing, and evaluation?

8. What are your experiences and expectations regarding collaboration by two or three provider organizations, and what are your conclusions regarding sustaining such collaborations by focusing attention on shared interests, complementary contributions, and equitable benefits?

9. Have your proposals included information on parts of the plan the reviewers might value as a basis for approving a request, such as needs, goals, activity, management, capability, budget details, project evaluation, and dissemination of results? Have your proposals explained contextual trends and influences that are likely to enhance project success and its continuation beyond external support?

PART FIVE

CONCLUSION

13

CONCLUSION
Making the 12 Tasks Work for You

It was a paradox. It emerged from evaluation results from many learning activities designed to enhance aspects of professional performance and quality improvement. Activity leaders differed in occupational roles and specialties, their provider organizations, and the extent of experience guiding professional learning sessions. They also varied in their session leadership, as assessed by participants and themselves, and as compared to published guidelines and external evaluations. The paradox was that excellent session leadership was only moderately associated with optimal conditions, session characteristics, and leader backgrounds.

However, my analysis of evaluations of actual sessions and related published concepts resulted in the 12 session leader tasks in this book. From six decades of helping to plan, conduct, and assess thousands of instances of helping adults learn, I have found that similar effective session leadership tasks recurred. This is especially so for members of helping professions seeking to enhance their occupational performance and to help the people they serve. Reviews of guidelines from related publications provided additional explanations of the leader process and guidelines, along with evidence of sustained performance improvements, thanks in part to stakeholder contributions.

Two broad themes regarding session dynamics emerged that helped explain effective sessions. One is the centrality of active engagement by participants. There is ample evidence that by itself online or face-to-face dissemination of content to passive participants is seldom associated with improved professional performance.

The second theme is that effective learning activity leaders, with varied experience and backgrounds, tend to discover and use leadership tasks—such as the examples in this book—to fashion guidelines for themselves that can result in increasing program effectiveness over the years. Such guidelines reflect the exemplars' experience, combined with concepts and conclusions from published reports. My intent is to share these concepts and examples and to suggest ways that people who help plan, guide, and evaluate professional learning activities can build on their experiences to continue to enhance the process and increase their creative enjoyment.

Effectiveness

Each of the 12 chapters deals with the effectiveness of professional learning activities. But what is the definition of *effective leadership of professional learning activities?* In addition to mastery of the distinctive content of each specialized field, leaders of professional development activities use methods and procedures to help participants learn. One indication of an effective session is that participants should be interactive to enhance their ability and commitment to improve their performance. The examples in each chapter were of leaders who were quite successful, and the concepts in each chapter help to explain why they were.

However, many of the people who conduct professional development sessions are less effective. The following five features are related to less effective sessions. The brief comments in parentheses at the end of each feature refer to a few applicable guidelines that could contribute to more successful results.

1. Sometimes a coordinator is asked to arrange a series of staff development activities for an improvement such as enhanced interpersonal relations. If offering this activity is mainly to respond to external expectations, if the coordinator is very busy, and information about the topic is presented in the familiar lecture style staff development activity, the resulting plans and learning activity are likely to be ineffective. (An alternative is for a coordinator to understand features of learning sessions that improve performance, such as emphasizing active learning and practice by participants, responding to participants' feelings and intentions, and providing ongoing evaluation feedback.)

2. Often busy professional development coordinators and leaders emphasize presentation of knowledge but neglect participants' attitudes about a topic. This may be because they are unfamiliar with more interactive learning methods, or it seems more efficient to them to use typical presentations a succession of busy session leaders could reuse when they conduct their next staff development session. (An alternative is for a coordinator, with one or two experienced program leaders, to clarify the intended outcomes to enhance professional performance and to plan

a sequence of interactive learning activities that encourage participants' commitment to apply what they learn.)

3. Some potential learning activity leaders are more likely to agree to conduct a staff development activity if they can present prepared content at an event without having to coordinate with other leaders and can apply that content to actual performance. If little program evaluation feedback occurs, leaders may not discover that declining participation reflects limited relevance. (An alternative is for the coordinator and leader to evaluate participants' experience and expectations and include interactive methods with continuity from session to session along with evaluation feedback before, during, and following activities.)

4. Many participants in staff development activities attend because of their assumptions about the combinations of program image, ease of access, reputation of leaders, activities, and potential benefits. They may think they can leave if the program does not seem worthwhile. If there are few connections between program activities and relevant applications and few opportunities to learn from other participants, they may not become engaged, even though they may remain at the sessions to avoid professional embarrassment. (An alternative is for event leaders to estimate diverse participant experience and expectations; provide options regarding relevant content, responsive activities, and materials; arrange opportunities for evaluation feedback to guide adjustments during a sequence of activities; and offer assistance during and following the program to enable participants to address combinations of personal and situational influences on performance and quality improvement.)

5. Professionals who plan, conduct, and evaluate professional learning activities may be unaware of the many concepts, examples, publications, print and electronic materials, and types of assistance with technology and evaluation that are available. Thus, they may proceed with a "death-by-PowerPoint," such as they may have experienced in the past. (An alternative is for leaders to explore ways to improve participants' performance by the efficient use of creative procedures that also enhance their own learning and future leadership of professional development activities.)

In contrast to these examples of insufficient planning, some less effective professional development activities can be overplanned in an effort to include as much content as possible in the time available. The typical result is mainly a presentation format, and often little time is left for questions and answers. A more creative and beneficial style would be to focus on a few topics that are relevant to the session leader and the participants. The leader could then use some of the answers from the original list of questions and topics as responses to participants' questions at the session. As a result of this interaction, the activity leader—as well as the participants—could gain from this creative experience by using some of what they learned.

Guidelines

The questions at the end of each chapter are intended to encourage readers to identify something on which to focus when leading professional learning activities, such as one of the following: responsiveness, creativity, performance, and evaluation.

1. *Be responsive.* The format of this book illustrates a way of assisting a professional learner to individualize his or her pursuit of a topic of interest. This book begins with my appreciation of diverse readers' experiences and expectations, which is explained in the preface, and an introduction that allows readers to become familiar with summaries of leader tasks; then presents short chapters with the main concepts and some examples to encourage readers to select a useful guideline; and ends with a bibliographic essay of evidence-based sources for readers interested in exploring specific topics in greater depth. This sequence is similar to responsive ways to guide seminars or tutorials.

2. *Be creative.* Many creative activities evolve over time as people who have a stake in the process and the outcomes of a creative activity interact with each other. This is a common feature of excellent practice in the helping professions. What people hope for and what actually occurs interact as people learn from their experience. The process as well as the outcomes are important.

3. *Enhance performance.* A central connection among professional learning leadership tasks is a widespread commitment to enhancing performance and quality improvement. In the helping professions, this is a team effort. Including relevant stakeholders in the process of planning and conducting learning activities can enhance the process and participants' commitment to use what is learned. Responsive and reflective sequences of active learning efforts contribute to the quality of the process and the outcomes.

4. *Provide evaluation feedback.* Ongoing efficient program evaluation feedback is central to planning, improvement, and accountability of professional learning activities. It is part of each leadership task, and in best practice it occurs before, during, and following learning activities. This

purposeful and reflective activity contributes to cooperation and excellent results. It is a central feature of the creative process in many fields.

Placing the bibliographic essay and reference list at the end of the book helps emphasize the value of reversing the usual sequence by beginning with diverse readers, introducing examples and concepts, and concluding with references to tested knowledge, compared with much of the preparatory education for young people that begins with presentation of knowledge and leaves it to students to make their applications in the future. Many of the people who lead professional learning activities are well prepared in the specialized content of their profession but typically are searching for concepts and examples to guide the learning process. Their experience doing so often gives rise to questions, some of which are answered by examples they discover from conversations with counterparts and from publications.

Many of the people I observed and interviewed for the examples included in this book are very effective and committed to excellent professional learning activities. They are also very busy. Years ago, as students, they may have dealt with long reading lists for graded courses but now prefer brief readings and inquiry. They use their experience, guided by examples, questions, and feedback. The participants in their professional development sessions appreciate their style and their responsiveness.

These leaders of effective professional learning activities seem to gain new insights from each session, which can enrich their future sessions. The participants appreciate their enthusiasm and commitment. Fortunately, some session leaders who value reflection and inquiry also share their experiences and conclusions in publications, which can enrich concepts and explanations of helping adults learn available to the rest of us.

The 12 chapters in this book are based on many concepts from experiences, observations, and publications regarding professional learning activities. Each section of this essay corresponds to one of the 12 chapters and includes multiple sources for applicability to various roles, fields, and teaching styles. Additional details are available from publications over many decades that can enhance planning of current professional learning. Each section also includes selected publications of special interest to leaders and coordinators. The references include a few early publications that helped shape major concepts and also many later publications that reflect current realities and suggest future directions. Those who are interested in publications related to a specific chapter can select publications that fit their experiences and plans from the sources in parentheses. The full list of references follows on page 121.

Chapter 1: Establishing Shared Purposes

Early stakeholder alignment of session goals and participant aspirations can increase activity leaders' responsiveness to creative opportunities, stakeholder expectations, options for individualization, recognition of influences, and future aspirations. During the past five decades, there have been repeated commentaries on past achievements related to learning (Houle, 1980; Knox, 1974; Manning & DeBakey, 1987) and future directions related to professional performance (Davis, Barnes, & Fox, 2003; Mott & Daley, 2000; Wentz, 2011). Such commentaries typically remark on the purposes of professional development, the separate professional fields, and quality improvement efforts (Sullivan, 2005). Houle (1980) concluded that 14 basic purposes of professional fields were relevant to continuing professional learning activities. A central function of professional learning sessions is to align the expectations of members of a profession and people who help them learn (Havelock, 1969; Houle, 1980). Broad professional development purposes can be linked to major program goals, session objectives, and individual expectations. Three general categories in a taxonomy of educational objectives are cognitive, affective, and psychomotor (Anderson & Krathwohl,

2001; Harrow, 1977). Professional development stakeholders can contribute to purposes, planning, conducting, and evaluating activities, with an emphasis on roles (Biddle & Thomas, 1966), negotiations (Cervero & Wilson, 2006), and coordination (Edelson, 1992). Effective activity leaders encourage participants to be innovative (Feldman, Csikszentmihalyi, & Gardner, 1994). Participant diversity can include professional fields and experience (Houle, 1980), social or personal roles (Biddle & Thomas, 1966), and gender (Friedan, 1964; Hayes & Flannery, 2000; Lively, 2013; Norris, 2010).

Chapter 2: Selecting Able Leaders

It has been well understood for decades that professional development coordinators can be more effective by using explicit criteria to select able people to guide professional learning activities (Houle, 1980; Knox, 1982; Manning & DeBakey, 1987). People in various roles use evaluation feedback about the effectiveness of the content and process of professional learning offerings and results. Green, Grosswald, Sutter, and Walthall (1984) reported quality indicators that were identified in various sites. In best practice, program coordinators and leaders who guide professional learning activities exemplify concepts similar to those of people who help adults learn in other settings (Kasworm, Rose, & Ross-Gordon, 2010; Peters & Jarvis, 1991). The effectiveness of professional development coordinators and session leaders is influenced by combinations of personal and situational influences, such as encouraging stakeholder reflection, providing options, and having a supportive organizational culture (Bennis, Goleman, & Toole, 2008; Cleveland, 1989). Effective activity leaders usually assess participants in various combinations of group and individualized activities (Heimlich & Norland, 1994; Knox, 1974; Pratt, 1998). People who effectively guide creative professional learning activities use such concepts and procedures to benefit participants during and after the activities (Sternberg, 2003). Career-long learning is a widely valued professional attribute.

Chapter 3: Being Responsive to Participants' Experiences and Expectations

Many concepts, examples, and guidelines are available to enable professional learning activity leaders to become increasingly responsive to diverse participants. Some publications focus on adult development and diversity (Bengston, 1996; Birren & Schaie, 1996; Findsen & Formosa, 2011) and some on adults as learners (Jarvis, 2006; Knox, 1977; Merriam, Caffarella,

& Baumgartner, 2007; Tennant, 2006). It is important to obtain, from participants and others, information about participants' educational needs and motives (Deci, 1975; Queeney, 1995; Wlodkowski, 2008). Pertinent characteristics of diverse participants are age and experience but especially educational level (Beatty & Wolf, 1996; Findsen & Formosa, 2011; Nelson & Bolles, 2010; Nuland, 2007; Rothwell, Sterns, Spokus, & Reaser, 2008). Participants also vary regarding multiple attitudes and abilities (Gardner & Walters, 1993; Goleman, 2006; Heidt, 2012). Many participants also differ regarding their preferences related to performance and organizational change, such as being conservers, originators, or pragmatists (Musselwhite, 2003). Similar distinctions regarding participant variation and responsiveness also apply to self-directed learning (Bandura, 1997; Brockett & Hiemstra, 1991; Deci, 1975; Hiemstra & Brockett, 1994; Johnson, 2001; Knox, 1974; Tough, 1979). One theme from these publications is that self-directed learners typically include interactions with other people in selective ways. Effective leaders work with multiple stakeholders to recognize various influences and select responsive methods.

Chapter 4: Specifying Current Participant Proficiencies

Estimating participants' current proficiencies may be enhanced if leaders recognize some useful distinctions, such as abilities (Gardner & Walters, 1993), feelings (Goleman, 2006; Heidt, 2012), and gender features (Hayes & Flannery, 2000; Lively, 2013; Norris, 2010). It is also desirable to address excellence and ethical concerns (Gardner, Csikszentmihalyi, & Damon, 2001; Sullivan, 2005). Concepts from such publications suggest questions that leaders can ask about participants' current proficiencies and can then use the answers to guide and assess activities (Gredler, 2006; Knowles, 1986; Moore, Green, & Gallis, 2009). Use of case examples can help participants and leaders better understand how things work (Barrows & Tamblyn, 1980; Merriam, 1988; Stake, 2010; Werner & DeSimone, 2009).

Chapter 5: Developing Shared Expectations

Several concepts can assist leaders to discover participant aspirations related to program activities, career development, and quality improvement. One is that participants can be guided to discover and recognize innovative ways to define problems and solutions (Aleckson & Ralston-Berg, 2011; Bateman, 1990; Cranton, 1996; Feldman et al., 1994; Osborn, 1953; Schön, 1987). Another is exposure to comparative analysis of similarities and differences between participants' typical professional performance and performance in other settings (Bauman, 2013; Bredeson, 2003; Bryson, 1988; Knox, 1993). Immersion in important societal issues (such as sustainability) can also help raise expectations (Robert, 2002). Professional learning activities can enhance participants' consciousness regarding success, abilities, and sources of wisdom (Cranton, 1996; Frederickson, 2009). An indicator that a professional development activity is attuned to participant expectations is when their comments and indications reflect a high level of engagement during and following sessions (Csikszentmihalyi, 1997; Havelock, 1969; Hiemstra, 1991; Sternberg, 1996, 2003). Clarification of participant expectations can contribute to decisions related to session purposes, procedures, and progress (Caffarella & Daffron, 2013; Johnson, 2001; Merriam, 1988; Queeney, 1995; Shattuck, 2014).

Chapter 6: Addressing Gaps Between Current and Desired Proficiencies

Effective leaders of professional learning activities help participants estimate discrepancies between participants' current and desired proficiencies to achieve alignment with learning activities and improved professional performance (Bateman, 1990; Bauman, 2013; Brookfield & Preskill, 1999; Davis et al., 2003). Such alignment is more likely to occur when participants and other stakeholders help narrow gaps related to current mastery as well as occupational opportunities and incentives (Gladwell, 2002). Sometimes the occupational development process entails negotiation, and professional learning activities can provide perspective and opportunities for practice and reflection (Fisher & Ury, 1991; Lewin, 1948). Specification and reflection related to explicit gaps can enable participants to use questions, examples, or simulations to narrow the discrepancies.

Chapter 7: Analyzing Situational Influences on Performance

Leaders can help participants recognize and analyze situational influences. Career development reflects a combination of situational and personal influences. Situational influences include complexity (Caffarella & Daffron, 2013; Cranton, 1996; Gladwell, 2002; Husén & Postlethwaite, 1985; Johnson, 2001; Kegan, 1994; Moore et al., 2009), changing cultural values (Hofstede, Hofstede, & Minkov, 2010; Kolb & Lewis, 1986), community issues (Boyte, 2004; Forester, 1989), and change events (Knox, 1977). Features of the workplace, such as quality improvement, can be especially influential on performance (Boud & Garrick, 1999; Bredeson, 2003; Davis et at., 2003; Lave & Wenger, 1991; Lynton & Elman, 1987; Pedler, 1991; Phillips & Stone, 2002; Quigley & Kuhne, 1997; Schein, 1985; Wenger, 2000; Werner & DeSimone, 2009). Strategies of primary care health clinics illustrate relations between personal and organizational influences (McBride et al., 2000). Effective demands and constraints related to organizational initiatives by professional development providers can influence the alignment between professional performance and organizational priorities (Beere, Votruba, & Wells, 2011; Sullivan, 2005). Increasing use of educational technology has contributed to societal (Greenblatt, 2011), organizational (Bates & Poole, 2003), and personal influences (Conceicao, 2011).

Chapter 8: Enhancing the Learning Transaction

Transactions between activity leaders and participants are the heart of professional learning and can take various forms. The basic concept is to align participant and leader expectations regarding learning activities (Knox, 1986). Kolb and Lewis (1986) apply such concepts to simulations for helping adults learn. Alignment guidelines are especially useful for multiple perspectives on teaching (Pratt, 1998). Such alignment also applies to individual coaching and mentoring (Daloz, 2012; Knowles, 1986; Wenger, 2000; Zachary, 2011). A rationale for alignment also applies to transactions related to changes in organizations (Argyris, 1993; Moore et al., 2009; Schmitz, 2011) and communities (Boyte, 2004; Robert, 2002). Effective activity leaders use quality indicators to plan, conduct, and evaluate transactions. An important ingredient in effective transactions is inclusion of reflection on beliefs and values (Schön, 1987). An early interest in art as experience soon expanded to include experience as art (Dewey, 1934; Knox, 2011).

For many decades, low-tech educational technology has been embraced as useful (Garrison, 1989; Verduin & Clark, 1991; Wedemeyer, 1981). Recent publications include more extensive use of computerized learning technology and simulations (Aldrich, 2009; Bates & Poole, 2003; Bauman, 2013; Conceicao, 2007, 2010, 2011; Flagg, 1990; Gredler, 2006). Diversity of participant familiarity with educational technology may entail use of both. Aleckson and Ralston-Berg (2011) analyzed collaboration between content experts and educational technology consultants. These concepts can be combined for specific occupational development purposes (Burge, Gibson, & Gibson, 2011; Daley & Cervero, 2014).

Connections among all 12 professional learning leadership tasks are especially important for effective transactions among leaders and participants. More than half a century ago, Myrdal (1944) explained a theory of a virtuous cycle of multiple influences on learning and social change, and Lindquist (1978) later expanded on the topic, focusing on multiple influences on faculty development and organizational change. A quarter of a century ago, Senge (1990) provided a similar explanation for organizations generally. Hess, Reed, Turco, Parboosingh, and Bernstein (2015) recently reported similar conclusions regarding multiple strategies for engagement of professionals in collaborative quality improvement in their work environment. Even for small-scale professional learning transactions among leaders and participants, attention to all 12 leader tasks can enhance professional performance, quality improvements, and benefits for people served by professionals (Davis et al., 2003; Sork, 2010).

Chapter 9: Using Active Methods With Participants

Effective leaders emphasize active engagement by participants regarding learning objectives, professional standards, and peer interactions (Bredeson, 2003; Caffarella & Daffron, 2013; Pedler, 1991; Pratt, 1998; Wenger, 2000). Participants should be actively engaged in professional learning activities and use what they gain for improved performance (Vella, 1994; Werner & DeSimone, 2009). From the many concepts and guidelines available, professional learning activity coordinators and leaders can select those that are allied with objectives and participants (Aldrich, 2009; Caffarella & Daffron, 2013; Houle, 1992; Kasworm et al., 2010; Moore et al., 2009). For some types of learning activities, active learning is especially central, such as active training and simulation (Argyris, 1993; Bauman, 2013; Silberman, 1998), inquiry (Bateman, 1990), action learning (Pedler, 1991), problem-based learning (Barrows & Tamblyn, 1980), discussion (Brookfield & Preskill, 1999), workshops (Fleming, 1997), and staff development (Daley & Cervero, 2014; Werner & DeSimone, 2009). Evaluation feedback can help session leaders use options (Bateman, 1990), subgroups (Brookfield & Preskill, 1999), technology (Caffarella & Daffron, 2013), supportive and challenging interactions (Knox, 2002), and individualized learning plans (Bateman, 1990) to be responsive to diverse participants. Technology can be used for very active engagement (Bauman, 2013; Caulfield, 2011; Conceicao, 2007, 2010, 2011; Flagg, 1990; Shattuck, 2014).

Chapter 10: Sequencing Activities for Progress

A central theme regarding planning and guiding professional learning activities is the connection between learning and occupational performance (Davis et al., 2003). Many publications on helping adults learn contain similar concepts about organization and evaluation of learning activities that enable participants to progress through individualization and reflection to enhanced performance (Caffarella & Daffron, 2013; Houle, 1996; Knox, 1986; Pratt, 1998). Self-directed learning projects also reflect considerations regarding sequencing (Brockett & Hiemstra, 1991; Moore et al., 2009; Tough, 1979). Additional concepts apply to hybrid courses (Caulfield, 2011).

Chapter 11: Providing Evaluation Feedback to Stakeholders

One application of program evaluation and feedback to stakeholders is assessment of results and benefits related to improved performance (Abrahamson, 1985; Brinkerhoff, 1987; Guskey, 2000; Hale, 2002; Knox, 2002; Phillips & Stone, 2002). Publications on evaluation of education, generally, and on continuing education of adults contain many concepts and examples applicable to professional development (Fitzpatrick, Sanders, & Worthen, 2004; Knox, 2002). Evaluation feedback can be used for stakeholder decisions regarding planning, improvement, and accountability about results that include enhancing professional performance (Angelo & Cross, 1993; Caffarella & Daffron, 2013; Queeney, 1995). Concepts regarding levels of successive stages of program evaluation focus on satisfaction and gain (Knox, 2002), performance (Hale, 2002), and benefits (Kirkpatrick & Kirkpatrick, 2006). Assessment of qualitative case studies can help explain how things work and provide guidelines regarding data collection and analysis (Gredler, 2006; Merriam, 1988, 2002; Miles & Huberman, 1984; Quigley & Kuhne, 1997; Stake, 2010). Half of the challenge of program evaluation is encouraging stakeholders to use the conclusions (Brinkerhoff, 1987; Patton, 2008). Effective leaders use their perspective on the connected tasks for guiding professional learning activities to select efficient and practical evaluation procedures that encourage participants' progress during and following learning events (Shattuck, 2014).

Leaders of professional learning activities who give some attention to all 12 leader tasks in their ongoing evaluation feedback to stakeholders, can receive several benefits. The first benefit is that for each evaluation activity focused on one or two tasks (such as shared aspirations, responsiveness, or active methods), the activity leader and coordinator will have available conclusions related to other tasks. The result is a systemic understanding of influences and effects to guide decisions for program planning and improvement. A second benefit of such metaevaluation is that leaders and scholars can use comprehensive explanations of how programs work for purposes of effective collaboration and connections between one educational activity and related concepts from relevant publications that provide the basis of such comprehensive explanations (Davis et al., 2003; Moore et al., 2009; Moore, 2013; Olson, Tooman, & Alvarado, 2010)

By coincidence, three publications in early 2015 contribute to a comprehensive rationale that includes multiple strategies for strengthening professional development activities that together can enhance professional performance and quality improvement. They do so from the vantage point of the enterprise where professionals work (Hess et al., 2015), universities (Bauchner & Fontanarosa, 2015), and a professional association (Shannon & Wiltenburg, 2015). Each publication includes multiple viewpoints about past experience, current realities, and future directions. They reinforce the utility of a systemic perspective that addresses multiple influences that can constitute a virtuous cycle, which over time contributes to personal and organizational change.

Chapter 12: Recognizing Contextual Influences

Program planning by professional development coordinators and session leaders can address organizational dynamics likely to affect their activity (Abrahamson, 1985; Caffarella & Daffron, 2013; Cervero & Wilson, 2006; Garrison, 1989). Leaders can also help create a climate for learning that is supportive and challenging (Hiemstra, 1991; Kegan, 1994; Knox, 1986; Vella, 1994). A brief version of strategic planning can help leaders identify external threats and opportunities to discuss as appropriate during an activity (Bryson, 1988; Forester, 1989; Knox, 1982). Sometimes planning and action is used to confront powerful resistance or at least issues to be negotiated (Lewin, 1948). International comparative analysis can sometimes illuminate local cultural differences for increased understanding (Aspin, Chapman, Hatton, & Sawano, 2001a, 2001b; Hofstede et al., 2010; Husén & Postlethwaite, 1985). For some potential improvements, it is useful to analyze and communicate diffusion of effective professional practices (Rogers & Agarwala-Rogers, 1971) and collaboration for production of technology-based simulations (Aldrich, 2009; Aleckson & Ralston-Berg, 2011).

Activity leaders can use their experience and organizational interactions to see more clearly how things work. Program planning stakeholders can use a systemic perspective for clarity and shared understanding (Cervero & Wilson, 2006; Katz & Kahn, 1966; Moore et al., 2009). Reports of comprehensive analysis can contain useful conclusions and implications (Green et al., 1984). Potential conclusions can include relations between the individual and the organization (Pedler, 1991; Schein, 1978; Werner & De Simone, 2009), situational learning (Lave & Wenger, 1991; Pedler, 1991; Sullivan, 2005; Wenger, 2000), and multiple influences (Lewin, 1948; Lindquist, 1978). Professional development efforts may entail either cooperation (Beder, 1984) or competition (Baden, 1987) among providers. Overviews can suggest to session leaders potential options and insights applicable to a specific setting (Davis et al., 2003; Lynton & Elman, 1987; Maehl, 2000).

Obtaining human and financial resources entails effective two-way communication among stakeholders (Havelock, 1969; Simerly, 1989). The activity leader's and coordinator's understanding of organizational culture can enhance cooperation (Phillips & Stone, 2002; Schein, 1985). Policymakers and administrators are in a strategic position to influence allocation of resources for professional development activities (Houle, 1997). Effective proposals for internal as well as external support can be central to the success of innovative activities (Buskey, 1981; Matkin, 1985; Simerly, 1993).

These references selected for each of the professional learning leadership tasks include more detailed explanations about relevant concepts and guidelines. They also contain additional ideas about professional development theory and practice over the years and emerging directions. Reading some of these publications can enrich your understanding and use of effective leadership strategies and encourage you to publish and share with your colleagues some of your experiences, evidence-enhanced conclusions, and suggestions.

REFERENCES

Abrahamson, S. (Ed.). (1985). *Evaluation of continuing education in the health professions*. Boston, MA: Kluwer-Nijhoff.

Aldrich, C. (2009). *Learning online with games, simulations, and virtual worlds*. San Francisco, CA: Jossey-Bass.

Aleckson, J. D., & Ralston-Berg, P. (2011). *Mindmeld: Micro-collaboration between eLearning designers and instructor experts*. Madison, WI: Atwood.

Anderson, L. W., & Krathwohl, D. (Eds.). (2001). *A taxonomy for learning, teaching, and assessing: A revision of Bloom's taxonomy of educational objectives*. New York, NY: Longman.

Angelo, T. A., & Cross, P. (1993). *Classroom assessment techniques* (2nd ed.). San Francisco, CA: Jossey-Bass.

Argyris, C. (1993). *Knowledge for action*. San Francisco, CA: Jossey-Bass.

Aspin, D., Chapman, J., Hatton, M., & Sawano, Y. (Eds.). (2001a). *International handbook of lifelong learning: Part one*. Boston, MA: Kluwer Academic.

Aspin, D., Chapman, J., Hatton, M., & Sawano, Y. (Eds.). (2001b). *International handbook of lifelong learning: Part two*. Boston, MA: Kluwer Academic.

Baden, C. (Ed.). (1987). Competitive strategies for continuing education. *New Directions for Continuing Education*, 35.

Bandura, A. (1997). *Self-efficacy*. New York, NY: Freeman.

Barrows, H. S., & Tamblyn, R. M. (1980). *Problem-based learning: An approach to medical education*. New York. NY: Springer.

Bateman, W. L. (1990). *Open to question: The art of teaching and learning by inquiry*. San Francisco, CA: Jossey-Bass.

Bates, T., & Poole, G. (2003). *Effective teaching with technology in higher education*. San Francisco, CA: Jossey-Bass.

Bauchner, H., & Fontanarosa, P. B. (Eds.). (2015). Professionalism, governance, and self-regulation of medicine. *JAMA, 313*(18): 1793–1794.

Bauman, E. (2013). *Game-based teaching and simulation in nursing and health care*. New York, NY: Springer.

Beatty, P., & Wolf, M. (1996). *Connecting with older adults*. Malabar, FL: Krieger.

Beder, H. (Ed.). (1984). Realizing the potential of inter-organizational cooperation. *Directions for Adult and Continuing Education*, 80.

Beere, C., Votruba, J., & Wells, G. (2011). *Becoming an engaged campus*. San Francisco, CA: Jossey-Bass.

Bengston, V. L. (Ed.). (1996). *Adulthood and aging: Research on continuities and discontinuities*. New York, NY: Springer.

Bennis, W., Goleman, D., & Toole, J. O. (2008). *Transparency: How leaders create a culture of candor*. San Francisco, CA: Jossey-Bass.

Biddle, B. J., & Thomas, E. J. (Eds.). (1966). *Role theory: Concepts and research*. New York, NY: Wiley.

Birren, J. E., & Schaie, K. W. (Eds.). (1996). *Handbook of the psychology of aging* (4th ed.). Orlando, FL: Academic Press.

Boud, D., & Garrick, J. (1999). *Understanding learning at work*. London, UK: Routledge.

Boyte, H. C. (2004). *Everyday politics: Reconnecting citizens and public life*. Philadelphia: University of Pennsylvania Press.

Bredeson, P. (2003). *Designs for learning: A new architecture for professional development in schools*. Thousand Oaks, CA: Corwin Press.

Brinkerhoff, O. (1987). *Achieving results from training: How to evaluate human resource development to strengthen programs and increase impact*. San Francisco, CA: Jossey-Bass.

Brockett, R. G., & Hiemstra, R. (1991). *Self-direction in adult learning: Perspectives on theory, research, and practice*. New York, NY: Routledge.

Brookfield, S., & Preskill, S. (1999). *Discussion as a way of teaching: Tools and techniques for democratic classrooms*. San Francisco, CA: Jossey-Bass.

Bryson, J. M. (1988). *Strategic planning for public and nonprofit organizations: A guide to strengthening and sustaining organizational achievement*. San Francisco, CA: Jossey-Bass.

Burge, E., Gibson, C., & Gibson, T. (2011). Flexible pedagogy: Notes from the trenches of distance education. Alberta, Canada: AU Press.

Buskey, J. H. (Ed.). (1981). Attracting external funds for continuing education. *New Directions for Continuing Education*, 12.

Caffarella, R., & Daffron, S. R. (2013). *Planning programs for adult learners: A practical guide* (3rd ed.). San Francisco, CA: Jossey-Bass.

Caulfield, J. (2011). *How to design and teach a hybrid course: Achieving student-centered learning through blended classroom, online and experiential activities*. Sterling, VA: Stylus.

Cervero, R. M., & Wilson, A. L. (2006). *Working the planning table: Negotiating democratically for adult, continuing, and workplace education*. San Francisco, CA: Jossey-Bass.

Cleveland, H. (1989). *The knowledge executive: Leadership in an information society*. New York, NY: NAL Dutton.

Conceicao, S. (2007). Teaching strategies in the online environment. *New Directions for Adult and Continuing Education*, 113.

Conceicao, S. (2010). *Creating a sense of presence in online teaching*. San Francisco, CA: Jossey-Bass.

Conceicao, S. (2011). *Managing online instructor workload*. San Francisco, CA: Jossey-Bass.

Cranton, P. (1996). *Professional development as transformative learning*. San Francisco, CA: Jossey-Bass.

Csikszentmihalyi, M. (1997). *Creativity: Flow and the psychology of discovery and invention.* New York, NY: HarperCollins.

Daley, B. J., & Cervero, R. M. (2014). Continuing professional education, development, and learning. In R. Poell, T. S. Rocco, & G. Roth (Eds.), *The Routledge companion to human resource development* (pp. 40–49). New York, NY: Routledge.

Daloz, L. A. (2012). *Mentor: Guiding the journey of adult learners* (3rd ed.). San Francisco, CA: Jossey-Bass.

Davis, D., Barnes, B., & Fox, R. (Eds.). (2003). *The continuing professional development of physicians.* Chicago, IL: AMA Press.

Deci, E. L. (1975). *Intrinsic motivation.* New York, NY: Plenum Press.

Dewey, J. (1934). *Art as experience.* New York, NY: Minton, Balch.

Edelson, P. (Ed.). (1992). Rethinking leadership in adult and continuing education. *New Directions in Continuing Education, 56.*

Feldman, D. H., Csikszentmihalyi, M., & Gardner, H. (1994). *Changing the world: A framework for the study of creativity.* New York, NY: Praeger.

Findsen, B., & Formosa, M. (2011). *Lifelong learning in later life.* Rotterdam, The Netherlands: Sense Publishers.

Fisher, R., & Ury, W. (1991). *Getting to YES: Negotiating agreement without giving in.* New York, NY: Penguin Books.

Fitzpatrick, J. L., Sanders, J. R., & Worthen, B. R. (2004). *Program evaluation* (3rd ed.). Boston, MA: Pearson.

Flagg, B. N. (1990). *Formative evaluation for educational technologies.* Hillsdale, NY: Erlbaum.

Fleming, J. A. (Ed.). (1997). New perspectives on designing and implementing effective workshops. *New Directions for Adult and Continuing Education, 76.*

Forester, J. (1989). *Planning in the face of power.* Berkeley: University of California Press.

Frederickson, B. (2009). *Positivity.* New York, NY: Three Rivers Press/Random House.

Friedan, B. (1964). *The feminine mystique.* New York, NY: Norton.

Gardner, H., Csikszentmihalyi, M., & Damon, W. (2001). *Good work: When excellence and ethics meet.* New York, NY: Basic Books.

Gardner, H., & Walters, J. (1993). *Multiple intelligences: The theory in practice.* New York, NY: Basic Books.

Garrison, D. R. (1989). *Understanding distance education.* New York, NY: Routledge.

Gladwell, M. (2002). *The tipping point: How little things can make a big difference.* New York, NY: Little, Brown.

Goleman, D. (2006). *Emotional intelligence: Why it can matter more than IQ.* New York, NY: Bantam Books.

Gredler, M. (2006). *Designing and evaluating games and simulations: A process approach.* Houston, TX: Guff.

Green, J. S., Grosswald, S. J., Sutter, E., & Walthall, D. B. (Eds.). (1984). *Continuing education for the health professions.* San Francisco, CA: Jossey-Bass.

Greenblatt, S. (2011). *The swerve.* New York, NY: Norton.

Guskey, T. R. (2000). *Evaluating professional development.* Thousand Oaks, CA: Corwin Press.

Hale, J. (2002). *Performance-based evaluation: Tools and techniques to measure the impact of training.* San Francisco, CA: Jossey-Bass.

Harrow, A. J. (1977). *A Taxonomy of the psychomotor domain.* New York, NY: Longman.

Havelock, R. G. (1969). *Planning for innovation.* Ann Arbor, MI: Center for Research on Utilization of Scientific Knowledge, Institute for Social Research, University of Michigan.

Hayes, E., & Flannery, D. (2000). *Women as learners: The significance of gender in adult learning.* San Francisco, CA: Jossey-Bass.

Heidt, J. (2012). *The righteous mind.* New York, NY: Pantheon.

Heimlich, J. E., & Norland, E. (1994). *Developing teaching style in adult education.* San Francisco, CA: Jossey-Bass.

Hess, D., Reed, V., Turco, M., Parboosingh, J., & Bernstein, H. (2015). Enhancing provider engagement in practice improvement. *Journal of Continuing Education in the Health Professions, 35*(1), 71–79.

Hiemstra, R. (Ed.). (1991). Creating environments for effective adult learning. *New Directions for Adult and Continuing Education,* 50.

Hiemstra, R., & Brockett, R. G. (Eds.). (1994). Overcoming resistance to self-direction in adult education. *New Directions for Adult and Continuing Education,* 64.

Hofstede, G., Hofstede, G. J., & Minkov, M. (2010). *Cultures and organizations.* New York, NY: McGraw-Hill.

Houle, C. O. (1980). *Continuing learning in the professions.* San Francisco, CA: Jossey-Bass.

Houle, C. O. (1992). *The literature of adult education.* San Francisco, CA: Jossey-Bass.

Houle, C. O. (1996). *The design of education.* San Francisco, CA: Jossey-Bass.

Houle, C. O. (1997). *Governing boards: Their nature and nurture.* San Francisco, CA: Jossey-Bass.

Husén, T., & Postlethwaite, T. N. (Eds.). (1985). *The international encyclopedia of education.* New York, NY: Pergamon Press.

Jarvis, P. (2006). *Towards a comprehensive theory of human learning.* New York, NY: Routledge.

Johnson, S. (2001). *Emergence: The connected lives of ants, brains, cities, and software.* New York, NY: Scribner.

Kasworm, C., Rose, A. D., & Ross-Gordon, J. M. (Eds.). (2010). *Handbook of adult and continuing education: 2010 edition.* Thousand Oaks, CA: Sage.

Katz, D., & Kahn, R. L. (1966). *The social psychology of organizations.* New York, NY: Wiley.

Kegan, R. (1994). *In over our heads: The mental demands of modern life.* Cambridge, MA: Harvard University Press.

Kirkpatrick, D. L., & Kirkpatrick, J. D. (2006). *Evaluating training programs: The four levels* (3rd ed.). San Francisco, CA: Jossey-Bass.

Knowles, M. S. (1986). *Using learning contracts: Practical approaches to individualizing and structuring learning.* San Francisco, CA: Jossey-Bass.

Knox, A. B. (1974). Life-long self-directed education. In R. J. Blakely (Ed.), *Fostering the growing need to learn* (pp. 65–131). Rockville, MD: Division of Regional Medical Programs, Bureau of Health Resources Development.

Knox, A. B. (1977). *Adult development and learning: A handbook on individual growth and competence in the adult years for education and the helping professions*. San Francisco, CA: Jossey-Bass.

Knox, A. B. (1982). Leadership strategies for meeting new challenges. *New Directions for Continuing Education*, 13.

Knox, A. B. (1986). *Helping adults learn: A guide to planning, implementing, and conducting programs*. San Francisco, CA: Jossey-Bass.

Knox, A. B. (1993). *Strengthening adult and continuing education: A global perspective on synergistic leadership*. San Francisco, CA: Jossey-Bass.

Knox, A. B. (2002). *Evaluation for continuing education: A comprehensive guide to success*. San Francisco, CA: Jossey-Bass.

Knox, A. B. (2011). Creativity and learning. *Journal of Adult and Continuing Education*, *17*(2), 96–111.

Kolb, D. A., & Lewis, L. H. (1986). Facilitating experiential learning: Observations and reflections. *New Directions for Continuing Education*, 30.

Lave, J., & Wenger, E. (1991). *Situated learning: Legitimate peripheral participation*. New York, NY: Cambridge University Press.

Lewin, G. N. (Ed.). (1948). *Resolving social conflicts: Selected papers on group dynamics (1935–1946)*. New York, NY: Harper.

Lindquist, J. (1978). *Strategies for change*. Berkeley, CA: Pacific Soundings Press.

Lively, P. (2013). *Dancing fish and ammonites*. New York, NY: Viking.

Lynton, E. A., & Elman, S. E. (1987). *New priorities for the university*. San Francisco, CA: Jossey-Bass.

Maehl, W. H. (2000). *Lifelong learning at its best*. Malabar, FL: Kreiger.

Manning, P., & DeBakey, L. (1987). *Medicine: Preserving the passion*. New York, NY: Springer Verlag.

Matkin, G. W. (1985). *Effective budgeting in continuing education*. San Francisco, CA: Jossey-Bass.

McBride, P. E., Underbakke, G., Plane, M., Massoth, K., Brown, R., Solberg, L., . . . Knox, A. (2000). Improving prevention systems in primary care practices: The Health Education and Research Trial (HEART). *Journal of Family Practice, 49*(2), 115–125.

Merriam, S. B. (1988). *Case study research in education: A qualitative approach*. San Francisco, CA: Jossey-Bass.

Merriam, S. B. (2002). *Qualitative research in practice: Examples for discussion and analysis*. San Francisco, CA: Jossey-Bass.

Merriam, S. B., Caffarella, R. S., & Baumgartner, M. (2007). *Learning in adulthood* (3rd ed.). San Francisco, CA: Jossey-Bass.

Miles, M. B., & Huberman, A. M. (1984). *Qualitative data analysis: A sourcebook of new methods*. Beverly Hills, CA: Sage.

Moore, D. E., Green, J. S., & Gallis, H. A. (2009). Achieving desired results and improved outcomes: Integrating planning and assessment throughout learning activities. *Journal of Continuing Education in the Health Professions, 29*(1), 1–15.

Moore, M. (Ed). (2013). *Handbook of distance education* (3rd edition). New York, NY: Routledge.

Mott, V. W., & Daley, B. J. (Eds.). (2000). Charting a course for continuing professional education: Reframing professional practice. *New Directions for Adult and Continuing Education*, 86.

Musselwhite, C. (2003). Managing change: Styles, stages, and effective leadership for academic leaders. In M. J. Johnson, D. E. Hanna, & D. Olcott (Eds.), *Bridging the gap: Leadership, technology, and organizational change for deans and department chairs* (pp. 55–74). Madison, WI: Atwood.

Myrdal, G. (1944). *An American dilemma*. New York, NY: Harper & Row.

Nelson, J., & Bolles, R. (2010). *What color is your parachute for retirement?* Berkeley, CA: Ten Speed Press.

Norris, M. (2010). *The grace of silence*. New York, NY: Vintage.

Nuland, S. B. (2007). *The art of aging: A doctor's prescription for well-being*. New York, NY: Random House.

Olson, C., Tooman, T., & Alvarado, C. (2010). Knowledge systems, health care teams, and clinical practice: A study of successful change. *Advances in Health Science Education*, *13*(1), 6–22.

Osborn, A. (1953). *Applied imagination*. New York, NY: Scribner.

Patton, M. Q. (2008). *Utilization-focused evaluation* (4th ed.). Thousand Oaks, CA: Sage.

Pedler, M. (Ed.). (1991). *Action learning in practice* (2nd ed.). Aldershot, UK: Gower.

Peters, J. M., & Jarvis, P. (1991). *Adult education: Evolution and achievements in a developing field of study*. San Francisco, CA: Jossey-Bass.

Phillips, J. J., & Stone, R. D. (2002). *How to measure training results: A practical guide to tracking the six key indicators*. New York, NY: McGraw-Hill.

Pratt, D. D. (1998). *Five perspectives on teaching in adult and higher education*. Malabar, FL: Krieger.

Queeney, D. (1995). *Assessing needs in continuing education: An essential tool for quality improvement*. San Francisco, CA: Jossey-Bass.

Quigley, B. A., & Kuhne, G. W. (Eds.). (1997). Creating practical knowledge through action research. *New Directions for Adult and Continuing Education*, 73.

Robert, K.-H. (2002). *The natural step story: Seeding a quiet revolution*. Gabriola Island, British Columbia, Canada: New Society Publishers.

Rogers, E. M., & Agarwala-Rogers, R. (1971). *Communication in organizations* (2nd ed.). New York, NY: Free Press.

Rothwell, W. J., Sterns, H. L., Spokus, D., & Reaser, J. M. (2008). *Working longer: New strategies for managing, training, and retraining older employees*. New York, NY: American Management Association.

Schein, E. H. (1978). *Career dynamics: Matching individual and organizational needs*. Reading, PA: Addison-Wesley.

Schein, E. H. (1985). *Organizational culture and leadership*. San Francisco, CA: Jossey-Bass.

Schmitz, P. (2011). *Everyone leads*. San Francisco, CA: Jossey-Bass.

Schön, D. A. (1987). *Educating the reflective practitioner*. San Francisco, CA: Jossey-Bass.

Senge, P. M. (1990). *The fifth discipline*. New York, NY: Doubleday.

Shannon, D. W., & Wiltenburg, R. (Eds.). (2015). *Centennial conversations: Essential essays in professional, continuing, and online education*. Washington, DC: University Professional and Continuing Education Association.

Shattuck, K. (Ed.). (2014). *Assuring quality in online education*. Sterling, VA: Stylus.

Silberman, M. (1998). *Active training: A handbook of techniques, designs, case examples, and tips*. San Francisco, CA: Jossey-Bass.

Simerly, R. G. (1989). *Handbook of marketing for continuing education*. San Francisco, CA: Jossey-Bass.

Simerly, R. G. (1993). *Strategic financing of conferences, workshops, and meetings*. San Francisco, CA: Jossey-Bass.

Sork, T. J. (2010) Planning and Delivering Programs. In C. E. Kasworm, A. D. Rose, A & J. M. Ross-Gordon (Eds.), *Handbook of adult and continuing education* (pp. 71–82). San Francisco: SAGE.

Stake, R. (2010). *Qualitative research: Studying how things work*. New York, NY: Guilford Press.

Sternberg, R. J. (1996). *Successful intelligence: How practical and creative intelligence determine success in life*. New York, NY: Simon & Schuster.

Sternberg, R. J. (2003). *Wisdom, intelligence, and creativity synthesized*. Cambridge, UK: Cambridge University Press.

Sullivan, W. (2005). *Work and integrity* (2nd ed.). San Francisco, CA: Jossey-Bass.

Tennant, M. (2006). *Psychology and adult learning* (3rd ed.). New York, NY: Routledge.

Tough, A. (1979). *The adult's learning projects: A fresh approach to theory and practice in adult learning* (2nd ed.). Toronto, Ontario, Canada: Ontario Institute for Studies in Education.

Vella, J. (1994). *Learning to listen, learning to teach: The power of dialogue in educating adults*. San Francisco, CA: Jossey-Bass.

Verduin, J. R., Jr., & Clark, T. A. (1991). *Distance education: The foundations of effective practice*. San Francisco, CA: Jossey-Bass.

Wedemeyer, C. A. (1981). *Learning at the back door*. Madison, WI: University of Wisconsin Press.

Wenger, E. (2000). *Communities of practice: Learning, meaning, and identity*. New York, NY: Cambridge University Press.

Wentz, D. (Ed.). (2011). *Continuing medical education*. Hanover, NH: Dartmouth College Press.

Werner, J., & DeSimone, R. (2009). *Human resource development*. Mason, OH: South-Western Learning.

Wlodkowski, R. J. (2008). *Enhancing adult motivation to learn: A comprehensive guide for teaching all adults*. San Francisco, CA: Jossey-Bass.

Zachary, L. (2011). *The mentor's guide: Facilitating effective learning relationships*. San Francisco, CA: Jossey-Bass.

ABOUT THE AUTHOR

Alan B. Knox is professor emeritus of educational leadership at the University of Wisconsin-Madison. Widely respected in the field, he twice received the American Association for Adult and Continuing Education's Imogene Okes Award for Outstanding Research in Adult Education, and has, over the years, authored or edited many books and *New Directions* quarterly sourcebooks, including such classic works as *Adult Development and Learning* (Jossey-Bass, 1977) and *Helping Adults Learn* (Helping Adults Learn, 1986). His book *Evaluation of Continuing Education: A Comprehensive Guide to Success* (Jossey-bass, 2002) received American Association for Adult and Continuing Education's (AAACE) Cyril O. Houle Award for Outstanding Literature in Adult Education. He continues his scholarly work and staff development sessions for helping professionals through the Office of Continuing Professional Development at the University of Wisconsin School of Medicine and Public Health.

Knox served as an administrator and faculty member at five universities in the United States (Syracuse University, University of Nebraska, Columbia University, University of Illinois, and University of Wisconsin). During his decade at Illinois, he was associate vice chancellor of academic affairs for continuing education and public service. He has been chair of the Commission of Professors of Adult Education, and president of AAACE. His book *Strengthening Adult and Continuing Education: A Global Perspective on Synergistic Leadership* (Jossey-Bass, 1993) was based on many case examples about dynamics and strategic planning of programs in more than 30 countries around the world. He was the initial editor-in-chief for the quarterly *New Directions in Adult and Continuing Education*, and edited a 1980 AAACE handbook. In recent years he has conducted keynote sessions and seminars in Hungary, Turkey, Canada, Scotland, and Taiwan. He lives in Madison, Wisconsin.

134 INDEX

professional development in, 65, 98–99
proficiency discrepancies and relicensure in, 49–50
human resource development (HRD), 21–22, 32, 94–95
humor, 16, 51, 71

indicators, 31, 63
of discrepancies, 52–53
of expectations, 44–46
of influences on learning, 93, 95–96, 101–2
for program development, 45–47
individual action plan, 14, 82
influences. See also contextual influences; organizational influences
on activities, 17–18, 97
assessment and understanding of, x, 5, 7, 18, 42, 45, 55, 58, 59, 65, 67, 69
on decision making, 38
on discrepancy reduction, 52, 54
diversity and, 2–3
examples of, 9, 56–57
external workplace, 55
globalization and, 17
indicators of, 93, 95–96, 101–2
leader identification of, 7, 17–18, 55, 58, 95–98, 101
leadership task on, 56, 94
on performance, 7, 15, 16, 27, 34, 53, 55–56
quality improvement and, 55, 58
role play to highlight, 57–59
innovation. See creative teaching and learning; creativity
interactive activities, 16, 83. See also peer interaction
for expectation inquiry, 43, 45, 107
performance enhancement with, 106
responsiveness during, 6, 108
technology with, 4, 67
transactions and, 8, 68

international practice, 9
interprofessional education, x, 56, 57–58, 88

journal clubs, 4, 33

knowledge. See proficiencies

leader-based indicators, 45, 46
leaders, activity, 2
active learning emphasis for, 70
apprenticeship for, 24
collaboration and, 56–57
developmental concepts for, 3
development of new, 25
discrepancy discovery by, 49–54
dual, effectiveness, 71–72
effectiveness of, ix–x, 22–23, 105–8
encouragement by, 44, 45, 47, 82–83
evaluation and feedback of, 45
guideline use by, 4, 66, 105–6
humor use by, 16, 51, 71
influences identification by, 7, 17–18, 55, 58, 95–98, 101
participant assessment by, 5–6, 25, 29, 32–33, 35, 45, 106–7
prior record of, 23–24
proficiency assessment by, 35–40
purpose alignment of, 15, 17–18
reflection questions for, 18–19, 25, 34, 39–40, 47, 54, 59, 68, 74–75, 82–83, 92, 101–2
responsiveness of, 5–6, 24, 29–31
words and choices of, 44
leader selection
coordinator's methods for, 21, 23–24
criteria for, 5, 22
proficiency understanding and, 22, 25
leadership, ix, x, 1, 2, 4, 22–23
leadership development program, 64
lifelong learning, ix, 1
logistics, 80

For Product Safety Concerns and Information please contact our EU
representative GPSR@taylorandfrancis.com
Taylor & Francis Verlag GmbH, Kaufingerstraße 24, 80331 München, Germany